MEANS TO AN END

MEANS TO AN END

U.S. Interest in the International Criminal Court

LEE FEINSTEIN

TOD LINDBERG

BROOKINGS INSTITUTION PRESS
Washington, D.C.

Library of Congress Cataloging-in-Publication data
Feinstein, Lee.
  Means to an end : U.S. interest in the International Criminal Court / Lee Feinstein and Tod Lindberg.
      p.   cm.
  Includes bibliographical references and index.
  Summary: "Reassesses U.S. relationship with the ICC and broader issues of U.S. policy toward international justice. Argues U.S. active support of ICC serves U.S. interests and is consistent with values to which America has aspired. Focuses on foreign policy, national security, and moral cases for shifting U.S. policy toward the Court"—Provided by publisher.
  ISBN 978-0-8157-0325-9 (hardcover : alk. paper) 1. International Criminal Court—United States. 2. International criminal courts—United States. 3. International criminal courts—Political aspects. 4. International cooperation. I. Lindberg, Tod. II. Title.
  KZ6311.F45 2009
  345'.01—dc22   2009030943

9 8 7 6 5 4 3 2 1

Printed on acid-free paper

Typeset in Sabon

Composition by Oakland Street Publishing
Arlington, Virginia

Printed by R. R. Donnelley
Harrisonburg, Virginia

CONTENTS

Contents

ACKNOWLEDGMENTS

We are grateful to the Brookings Institution for sponsoring this project on U.S. policy toward international justice and the International Criminal Court. The institution had the foresight to see the opportunity for reframing the debate on an issue that goes to the heart of American values and national interest.

We wish to thank Brookings President Strobe Talbott for his enthusiastic backing of this effort, including both his intellectual input and his willingness to provide an institutional home for Lee Feinstein. We are grateful for the support of Brookings Vice President and Director of Foreign Policy Studies Carlos Pascual and Senior Fellow and Deputy Director of Foreign Policy Ted Piccone, as well as Brooking Institution leaders William Antholis and Steven Bennett. We are also grateful to the Hoover Institution and its director, John Raisian, for ongoing support of Tod Lindberg and for the use of Hoover's Washington office for meetings and discussion groups.

We were lucky to have agile foundations willing to support our work. This project would not have been possible without the generosity of the Jolie-Pitt Foundation, and the personal support of Angelina Jolie and Trevor Neilson. We also received major funding from Humanity United and wish especially to thank Peter Rundlet, Tarek Ghani, and Dave Mozersky. The Connect U.S. Fund provided seed money for this project through its quick reaction fund and stimulated other giving. We are especially grateful to Eric Schwartz and Francesco Femia. We would also like to thank Ambassador Renée Jones-Bos of the Netherlands, whose early interest in this project was a substantial resource. Newt Gingrich and George Mitchell, though not involved in this project, facilitated the fruitful collaboration of the co-authors on the U.S. Institute of Peace's Task Force on American Interests and UN Reform, which they chaired. We have tried to build here on its work in forging a nonpartisan approach to America's proper role in international institutions.

We were fortunate in writing this book to have the support of an outstanding, dedicated, and diverse group of policy practitioners, legal experts, and academics who helped us on a nonpartisan basis to work through the details of the important and challenging issues of international justice and the International Criminal Court. We established an informal advisory group, which met twice over the course of six months. Many of the members generously prepared background papers for us and were extraordinarily giving of their time in providing commentary on the manuscript at various stages. This was not a consensus project, and we are certain that all members of the advisory group will not be in accord with all the conclusions presented here. But our project was strengthened by the challenges members posed as well as the nuances of the support we received. We thank Kenneth

Anderson, Lieutenant Colonel Jane-Ellen Bagwell, Gary Bass, John Bellinger, William Burke-White, Christine Chung, Eugene Fidell, Jack Goldsmith, Colonel William Lietzau, Colonel Peter Mansoor, Elisa Massimino, Madeline Morris, David Rivkin, Kenneth Roth, David Scheffer, Major General Douglas Stone, Peter Singer, Lieutenant Colonel Robert Vasquez, Benjamin Wittes, and Ruth Wedgwood. Others who contributed, either by advising us or granting interviews, we are unable to thank by name. Special thanks to Brookings Senior Fellow Michael O'Hanlon, a great colleague who both participated in the advisory group and helped shepherd this book to publication.

Matthew Hall provided invaluable research assistance and administrative leadership for the project while at Brookings and thereafter. Daniel Belkin contributed first-rate research on the American historical record on international justice. Teresa Lewi probed the extent to which the Pentagon collects relevant statistics on accountability. Alex Little, who previously worked in the prosecutor's office at the International Criminal Court, combined an insider's perspective on the operation of the Court and a lawyer's knack for framing an argument persuasively. We are in their debt.

We are grateful for the enthusiasm of the Brookings Institution Press and its fine and professional team, including Robert Faherty, Jaime Fearer, Christopher Kelaher, Tom Parsons, Janet Walker, and Susan Woollen. Thanks to our copy editor, Janet Mowery, for her signal contribution in improving the manuscript. Any errors that remain are on us, not those mentioned above.

Finally, we wish to thank Tina Lindberg and Elaine Monaghan and their and our children, Abby and Molly Lindberg and Jack and Cara Feinstein, all staunch supporters of us and our work.

MEANS TO AN END

CHAPTER ONE

THE OPPORTUNITY

THE TIME IS AT HAND for a major reassessment of the relationship between the United States, the International Criminal Court, and the broader issue of U.S. policy toward international justice. Long opposed by the senior U.S. military leadership, signed onto only with grave reservations by the United States during the administration of President Bill Clinton, and ceremoniously unsigned by the administration of President George W. Bush, the ICC has been a political third rail in the United States. Yet recent developments in Washington, New York, and The Hague suggest that a policy of formal U.S. government opposition to the Court may yield to a policy of de facto acceptance and, we hope, active U.S. cooperation with the Court in its important mission.

The turning point for a broad policy shift in the United States was little appreciated when it occurred. In March 2005, without fanfare, rather than veto a UN Security Council resolution referring allegations of war crimes in Darfur, Sudan, to the ICC, as many expected, the United States abstained, allowing the referral to go through. Although hardly an expression of newfound affection for the ICC, let alone a willingness to re-sign the Rome Statute creating the Court, the abstention by the Bush administration did acknowledge for the first time its recognition of the Court's utility in an actual case of international justice. Properly understood, which it has not been, the Darfur referral constituted an important precedent for the U.S. government and the international community. That initial abstention was followed by several noteworthy actions by the Bush administration and, since then, the administration of Barack Obama: senior Bush administration officials, from the State Department's chief legal adviser to the U.S. permanent representative to the United Nations, took the opportunity to reaffirm U.S. support for the work of the ICC prosecutor in the Darfur case. Officials from the Bush administration repeatedly expressed U.S. opposition to a proposal that the UN Security Council postpone the possible ICC indictment of Sudan's president, Omar al-Bashir, an option the Sudanese government was actively pursuing through diplomatic channels—an indication of the seriousness with which the Court's activities are taken by perpetrators with little or nothing to fear from local judicial systems, and therefore of the leverage the ICC brings to the rights-regarding elements of the international community in its dealings with the world's worst human rights abusers.

The Bush administration's emergence as a principal defender of letting justice run its course—a position supported by the Obama administration—ironically has put the United States at odds with other members of the Security Council, including parties to the Rome Statute, who cite concern about damage to unfruitful peace negotiations that have dragged on for many years. But there can be no question that the ICC's engagement has substantially increased the pressure on the Sudanese government.

This turn of events does not constitute a role reversal for the United States and Europe on the ICC, even in a new administration. It is, for example, difficult to envision early advice and consent to ratification of the ICC. During the presidential campaign, neither nominee, in fact, committed the United States to joining the Court (although both emphasized the need for the United States to take a leading international role in preventing and stopping mass atrocities).

What these events do mean is that many Americans, as a matter of conscience, principle, and national interest, believe it is time to end America's policy of formal hostility to the Court and replace it with a clear and unequivocal policy to support the Court in its important mission of bringing perpetrators of mass atrocities to justice.[1]

This is a principle embraced by the Obama administration, and one with historical roots. The authors glimpsed the first signs of cross-ideological support for this premise during the Bush administration in their work on the 2005 congressionally mandated U.S. Institute for Peace task force on U.S.–UN relations, co-chaired by former House speaker Newt Gingrich and former Senate majority leader George Mitchell. That task force did not seek to reach consensus on the ICC, nor would it have been able to, but its members understood the significance of their unanimous recommendation, unprecedented for a group of prominent Democrats and Republicans, that "perpetrators must be held accountable for war crimes and crimes against humanity."[2]

Another, more recent, bipartisan report went further still: the Genocide Prevention Task Force, a privately funded project of the U.S. Holocaust Memorial Museum, the U.S. Institute of Peace, and the American Academy of Diplomacy, co-chaired by former secretary of state Madeleine Albright and former secretary of defense William S. Cohen, included among its recommendations a call for reaffirmation of the principle of non-impunity, further elaborating: "Although the stated concerns of the U.S. government preclude the United States from becoming a party to the Rome Statute at present, the United States must acknowledge, embrace, and build on the emerging modus vivendi between the U.S. government and the ICC." This was the first major bipartisan statement in support of building a positive relationship between the United States and the Court.[3]

Finally, following our work on the Gingrich-Mitchell task force, the two of us began to try to think through the implications of the Darfur referral to the ICC. Having consulted extensively with U.S., UN, and European officials in Washington, New York, Brussels, The Hague, and Geneva both in the run-up to the Darfur referral and in its aftermath, we concluded that the potential significance of the referral was underappreciated both at home and abroad. Through the Council on Foreign Relations, we approached the John D. and Catherine T. MacArthur Foundation (among others) to explore its interest in supporting a project on U.S. relations with the ICC.[4] We discovered that MacArthur's grantmaking strategy for ICC matters allowed for support for work on the ICC abroad, but not in the United States, according to the reasoning that the U.S. debate on the Court was so polarized and politicized that no meaningful work was likely to result. Based on the preliminary research we had done, we set about to persuade the foundation otherwise—either to change its strategy or to allow for an exception in this case, on account of changing circumstances. This effort was ultimately successful. However, shortly before we had proposed to begin work, one of us accepted a position with a presidential campaign, and we agreed to defer our joint research until we were mutually available.[5] In the interim, however, the MacArthur Foundation funded an independent, bipartisan task force convened by the American Society for International Law (ASIL), co-chaired by William H. Taft IV and Patricia M. Wald. Its report, issued in March 2009, recommended "engagement with the ICC and the Assembly of States Parties in a manner that enables the United States to help further shape the Court into an effective accountability mechanism. The Task Force believes that such engagement will also facilitate future consideration of whether the United States should join the Court." We were pleased to share the first draft of this book with some members of the ASIL task force as it was preparing its report and recommendations.

Building a sustainable basis for ending U.S. hostility to the Court, and adopting instead a policy of cooperation in support of its mission, requires a reframing of the debate about the Court that can build on the bipartisan spirit of Gingrich-Mitchell, the Genocide Prevention Task Force, and contributions from the legal community such as the ASIL report. In the past, proponents of the Court have often led with the argument that the United States needs to subordinate itself to an international institution, asserting broad jurisdiction without clarity about the benefits to the United States. For many supporters, the frame of the ICC debate was "global governance," a matter of some controversy for a nation with a vast military, extensive global responsibilities, and a historically ingrained proclivity for zealous protection of its own sovereign rights. Largely absent from the global governance perspective, if not from the formal U.S. government statements on the matter, was clarity about the return benefits to U.S. national interests and American values of participation in the Court.[6]

With this book we reframe the discussion on the International Criminal Court in two ways. First, we broaden the focus to address not simply the International Criminal Court, but the broader issue of U.S. policy toward international justice. The International Criminal Court is a court of last resort—a potential means to the end of putting the perpetrators of mass atrocities behind bars where no other option exists. Accordingly, the role of the ICC in U.S. foreign policy should be evaluated in the context of the degree to which it helps to bring *génocidaires* and other war criminals to justice. Second, we focus on the foreign policy, national security, and moral case for shifting U.S. policy toward the Court—not on the important but, for these purposes, tangential question of global governance. This book evaluates the ICC by the degree to which it advances the interests of international justice, which the United States has supported enthusiastically, imperfectly, and at times skeptically over its 250-year history.

We note that the pursuit of "justice" in this sense is not and never will be the only goal of U.S. foreign policy, nor the only goal of an American foreign policy that aspires to be morally worthy. Other ends are important as well, ranging from the pursuit of peace in situations of conflict to the protection of vital interests. These ends sometimes come into conflict, and it is not always possible to avoid trade-offs. But we do say that no American foreign policy is complete any more without due regard for justice, and it is as a means to the pursuit of justice as an important end of U.S. policy, not necessarily as the sole end of U.S. policy, that we ought to be looking at the ICC.

Toward that aim, we address five areas. First, we remind readers that the United States has a long, though hardly perfect, record in support of the advance of human and political rights and the proposition that violators of those rights and perpetrators of mass atrocities should be held to account for their actions. The term "international justice" is relatively new, but the ideas that underlie it are not. The questions posed by participation in the ICC do not come out of a vacuum. They arise, above all, from the unwillingness of the rights-regarding members of the international community to accept impunity for perpetrators of mass atrocities in the name of sovereign right.

Paradoxically, the United States, as a zealous guardian of sovereign rights, is uniquely well positioned to demonstrate through argument and deed that with sovereign rights come sovereign responsibilities of the sort recognized in the protections afforded Americans in their own founding documents. At the heart of these is, quite simply, the right to live. A sovereign power that fails to protect this most basic right is failing its most basic obligation.[7] And a leader of a state or a political movement or an armed gang whose activities include the perpetration of genocide, crimes against humanity, and war crimes deserves to be held to account.

Second, we describe the elements of the Court most ardently criticized by its opponents and trace the elements that led the Bush administration to adopt a policy of acquiescence toward the Court. In doing so, we reinforce support among activist groups and religious and other communities from the political left and right for the principle of prosecuting war crimes, and make the foreign policy and national security arguments that led the United States to realign its position.

Third, we assess the operation of the ICC since it entered into force in 2002. We evaluate the performance of the Court against the various scenarios envisioned by critics of U.S. membership or cooperation and consider the degree to which the ICC, established as a Court of last resort, has succeeded in promoting capacity and will in states and regions to prosecute cases themselves, without appeal to an international institution, and what steps the Court—

in concert with other actors, including the United States—can take to promote the building of local capacity.

Fourth, we take up the question of U.S. national interests. We touch on the foreign policy consequences of a U.S. posture that has opposed the Court, including the impact on relations with close allies, military partners, and America's overall international reputation among rights-regarding members of the international community. We consider what the costs of continued opposition might be internationally and weigh those costs against the supposed benefits of U.S. opposition in light of the Court's history and practice to date. We explain the potential benefits to Americans of greater participation in and cooperation with the Court and look candidly at concerns about the costs of U.S. participation and the ways in which such concerns can be mitigated and the costs reduced. In the conclusion we call for the United States to end a policy of opposition or hostility toward the Court and to adopt instead a policy of cooperation to help the Court with its important work of bringing the most heinous perpetrators of war crimes to justice.

Finally, we make recommendations for the United States to act on legislatively and within the Executive Branch to advance a policy of cooperation, including how the United States should develop a productive working relationship with the Court short of ratification of the Rome Statute—a decision we do not think will be ripe for consideration before the conclusion of the 2010 Review Conference of the Rome Statute. The interim period will give the United States and the Court time to adopt a pattern of cooperation and a basis for Washington to decide on next steps.

Most fundamentally, *A Means to an End* argues that the United States should actively support the International Criminal Court, not as an act of international charity, not as a project of "global governance," not even principally to send a strong message of international cooperation to our close allies and others (though adoption of our proposal will send such a message). This book argues that the United States should support the Court because it serves our interests and is consistent with the values that animated the founding of the country, and to which we continue to aspire.

CHAPTER TWO

U.S. HISTORY AND INTERNATIONAL JUSTICE:

Idealism and Ideology

MANY OF THE CONCERNS that have arisen over the Rome Statute that created the International Criminal Court were previewed in halting U.S. support for a variety of international judicial schemes dating back to the Civil War and beyond. Concerns about surrendering sovereignty to an international judicial body have long been in competition with an American impulse to foster the rule of law everywhere.

Idealistic schemes were proposed and opposed by successive U.S. government officials over the years. Europe and the United States frequently exchanged roles as the main proponents of or skeptics about various judicial proposals. Over the course of a century and a half, the United States has been at the heart of efforts to establish rules governing the conduct of war; has supported with varying degrees of intensity efforts to establish an international criminal court; and has led international efforts to establish the principle of individual accountability (the

Nuremberg principles, undermined to an extent by the over-militarized and inconsistent Tokyo tribunals that followed). But the United States has also generated profound skepticism about the prospects of securing anything like "international justice" or global governance more broadly—a product of the very basic concern that the pursuit of international justice will jeopardize the ability of a free people to pursue justice as they see fit in a sovereign and democratic state that fought a war for independence against an oppressive king. In this view, global governance of uncertain legitimacy will seek to trump democratic and constitutional national governance. At its best, U.S. efforts to advance human rights and political freedom have blended pragmatism with the aspirational values on which the country was founded.

In a 1995 speech delivered at the University of Connecticut, President Bill Clinton said, "We have an obligation to carry forward the lessons of Nuremberg. That is why we strongly support the United Nations War Crimes Tribunal for the former Yugoslavia and for Rwanda."[1] Although this statement may have overstated initial U.S. enthusiasm for the International Criminal Tribunal for the former Yugoslavia (ICTY), in harking back to America's leadership in promoting international justice fifty years earlier the president sought to affirm the United States' aspiration, if not always practice, to stand as a global champion of international justice. Yet just three years later in Rome, owing to opposition to some of the most basic aspects of how the new International Criminal Court would operate, the Clinton administration found itself voting with only a handful of other nations against the treaty language. Clinton eventually signed the Rome Statute—but with the stated intention not to submit the treaty to a highly skeptical Senate for approval until its defects could be corrected. Both the aspiration and the hesitation were very much of a piece with the American historical record.

During the U.S. Civil War, American legal scholars codified the first modern laws of war that fostered humanitarianism on the battlefield and subsequently served as the jurisprudential basis for prosecuting culpable offenders—though at first aimed primarily at the atrocities of the Confederacy, not the Union. The United States was the driving force behind the creation of the Nuremberg and Tokyo tribunals that put World War II war criminals on trial—though of course few Americans would have stood for or been able to conceive of an international war crimes investigation of Allied conduct during the war. Washington in the 1990s led the international community once again in constructing global judicial mechanisms, this time to target the liable generals and *génocidaires* of Yugoslavia and Rwanda. But at the same time, concerns about actual and potential infringement of U.S. sovereignty roiled domestic politics.

In looking at the broad picture, however, America has more often than not demonstrated fidelity to the core principle of international justice: war criminals should not receive impunity for their horrendous actions.

Founding Aspirations

America's Declaration of Independence was self-consciously intended as a global manifesto as well as a national one. The principles of the eighteenth-century Enlightenment—law, liberty, progress, and reason—came to serve as the basis for twentieth-century international justice. In 1625, the Dutch jurist Hugo Grotius, the grandfather of international law, articulated the natural rights of human beings in the context of law.[2] In its revolutionary assertion of natural rights, the Declaration of Independence affirmed that the U.S. government in theory if not in practice was established to reflect the equality, universality, and naturalness of rights.

As such, the nascent United States became the rhetorical standard-bearer of the Enlightenment. This self-awareness shaped the outlook of the United States toward the rest of the world. Americans "believed their own fate was in some way tied to the cause of liberalism and republicanism both within and beyond their borders."[3] Benjamin Franklin asserted that America's "cause is the cause of all mankind." John Adams remarked that the colonies waged the rebellion "as much for the benefit of the generality of mankind in Europe as for their own." Thomas Jefferson wrote that the westward expansion of the new nation would advance liberal ideals, in keeping with an American ethos that the global spread of republican institutions and the upending of tyrannies would bring a more peaceful and prosperous world. He and other founders saw the French Revolution as part of this global movement. John Marshall said: "I sincerely believed human liberty to depend in a great measure on the success of the French Revolution."[4] In sum, the framers asserted they had a national interest in the ideological upheavals unfolding beyond America's shores.

Of course, the rhetorical promises to export the values of the American Revolution abroad did not extend to large segments of society at home, including slaves, other non-whites, Native Americans, and women. The notions of "women's rights" and political equality were radical when they came up at all.[5]

Suppression of Piracy and Defense of Free Trade

In the decades following its founding, the United States also positioned itself as a promoter of the freedom of the seas and free trade. In defending these principles, America emerged as an active opponent of piracy in the early nineteenth century. Pirates were seen as operating in direct opposition to the laws of nations and norms of the civilized world.[6] The freedom of the seas served U.S. national interests, allowing America as an expanding seafaring nation to engage safely in commerce.

Overarching the discussion of maintaining the freedom of the seas was the American aspiration for free trade. Once constrained by the yoke of British mercantilism, post-independence Americans sought unfettered access to distant markets and freedom from trade restrictions. From this perspective, the same natural rights of liberty and equality outlined in the Declaration of Independence would govern U.S. commercial relations with the outside world. Free trade was the logical outward behavior of the free and dynamic society being built at home in the United States. Contemporaries harbored convictions in the correlation between free commerce among nations and transnational peace: economic interaction would help foster political harmony. "Americans viewed the pirates as a vestige of an unenlightened and vanishing time when depredations of power, not the rule of law, dictated the rhythms of trade."[7]

THE LIEBER CODE AND THE
BROADER CODIFICATION OF THE LAWS OF WAR

The nineteenth century witnessed the emergence of an international movement to codify the laws of war. The United States played a role in promoting this jurisprudential movement. The mass production of the Industrial Revolution had forever altered the character of modern warfare. Battlefield combat had been totalized into mass industrial slaughter: a man-made catastrophe.

Jurists posited that the application of Enlightenment values on the field of battle would promote a humanitarian ethos and thwart wartime atrocities. With the American Civil War as the first truly modern war, President Abraham Lincoln selected Columbia College professor Francis Lieber to develop rules of land warfare to guide the Union armies. The subsequent Lieber Code became U.S. law in April 1863 and detailed a broad range of constraints, including conduct in guerrilla warfare, the treatment of captured enemy soldiers, and the handling of enemy property.[8] The Lieber Code was the first concrete legal framework in Western history created to regulate an actual war—a watershed in the history of law and war.[9]

At the conclusion of the horrific conflict, the United States set out to rebuke the violators of the new laws of war. For this emerging era of legalism in warfare, the flouting of laws required due prosecution and punishment—just as in civilian society. Georgia's infamous Andersonville prison camp earned northern wrath against the vanquished Confederacy. Designed to hold 10,000 inmates, the Andersonville prison population ballooned to 33,000 by August 1864. Interned Union soldiers died by the thousands owing to malnourishment and inhospitable conditions. Upon learning of the horrendous details, Secretary of War Edwin Stanton responded passionately, but in the language of law: "The enormity of the crime committed by the rebels cannot but fill with horror the civilized world."[10]

In consequence, a Union military commission in August 1865 indicted Henry Wirz, the commandant of Andersonville, for war crimes. Domestic military courts were the conventional venue at the time for the prosecution of war criminals. The majority of the charges centered on Wirz's deliberate murder and abuse of prisoners in wanton violation of the Lieber Code. In October 1865, the military court ruled that the commandant was guilty of "conspiring . . . against the United States, against the laws of war, to impair and injure the health, and to destroy large numbers of Federal prisoners." He subsequently was sentenced to death and was hanged in November 1865. The trial of the commandant stood as a modern landmark in the legal regulation of war. In the following decades, the groundbreaking American statute became the blueprint for European efforts to codify their own laws of war.[11]

The Lieber Code did not, however, protect Native Americans under siege from U.S. soldiers in the American West. While Union prisoners were suffering at Andersonville, in November 1864, 700 U.S. soldiers slaughtered 28 men and 105 women and children of the Cheyenne and Arapaho tribes at Sand Creek in Colorado. The same laws governing the treatment of Confederates—white Americans—failed to shield the "savages" in the American West from cruelty.[12] In contrast to the fate of the commandant of Andersonville, no one was held responsible for the massacre at Sand Creek. Non-white peoples still were excluded from the liberalism of the United States.

By the late nineteenth century, the United States' original endeavor to contain the horrors of modern war through legal means had spread to Europe. Delegates from twenty-six nations, including the United States, convened in The Hague, the Netherlands, in 1899. The resulting multilateral accord specified rules on the treatment of prisoners, casualties, and spies as well as detailing procedures for capitulation and neutrality. The legal paradigm the Lieber Code introduced was broadened in scope. The American representatives were more ambitious than their European counterparts at The Hague. The United States proposed the creation of the Permanent Court of Arbitration that would resolve disputes between states in hopes of preventing needless bloodshed. Rather than simply placing parameters around the waging of war, the American delegation put forth bold (often overreaching) designs to revolutionize the way international relations were conducted. The United States wanted to mitigate the menace of international anarchy with a super-sovereign institution. The proposed international court of arbitration reflected the objective, as explained by American delegate Joseph Choate, to render war "an anachronism, like dueling or slavery, something that international society had simply outgrown."[13] The Hague Convention of 1899 catalyzed optimism in the West that the power of law would usher in a more peaceful twentieth century.

At the behest of President Theodore Roosevelt, forty-four nations gathered once again at The Hague in 1907 to revise the first Hague Convention. The second summit boasted of the same mission: to "serve the interests of humanity and the ever progressive needs of civilization by diminish[ing] the evils of war." The general laws and customs of war were expanded from the 1899 Hague Conference.[14] In addition, the United States aspired to enhance the scope of the new Permanent Court of Arbitration. The secretary of state encouraged the American delegation to advance "international justice and peace." Choate remarked at the global summit, "And so at last, after three centuries, will be realized the dream of Grotius, the founder of international law, that all civilized nations of the earth will submit to its dictates, whether in war or peace."[15]

Despite the lofty rhetoric supporting international jurisprudential structures, no participant, including the United States, harbored any willingness to create an institution that would hold *individual* war criminals to account. In adherence to precedent, domestic courts would remain responsible for enforcing the laws of war.[16] There were limits to the American willingness to submit to international bodies.

The Paris Peace Conference 1919:
War Crimes Trials and the Fourteen Points

In the face of the unparalleled scope and shocking brutality of the Great War, the United Kingdom and France crafted elaborate judicial designs to bring Germany's Kaiser Wilhelm II and other accused war criminals to account. Over the course of the four-year slog, Germany unleashed merciless tactics on the land, at sea, and in the air that repulsed the moral consciences of the Allies. The conduct of Germany, including unlimited submarine warfare and the strategic air bombing of London, shattered the humanitarian hopefulness and idealism that had been building along legal lines over the preceding century. The spirit of the Hague Conventions was undone.[17] In the eyes of the Allies, the barbarism of Germany signified a treacherous regression into medievalism: the twentieth century could not tolerate a return to fourteenth-century ideas about acceptable conduct in wartime.

As a result, from the British perspective, the Teutonic assault on Enlightenment values would be parried with the reinforcement of those principles. The British and French delegations at the 1919 Paris Peace Conference pressed the Allies to allow for unprecedented multinational tribunals to punish German war criminals, including the Kaiser, for their atrocities. In January 1919 the Allies established the Commission on the Responsibilities of the Authors of War and on Enforcement of Penalties. Its purview was to ascertain guilt for the authorship of the Great War and for the war crimes committed. Over the next two months, British and American delegations clashed over the proper venue for the judicial punishment of the Germans. This time it was the American side resisting the forward-leaning British. The secretary of state maintained that there was no precedent for trying heads of state for crimes committed by their subordinates: the trial of the Kaiser would violate the legal precept of ex post facto. In addition, according to the Americans, the notion of "laws and principles of humanity" articulated by the commission was too vague to be judicially salient.[18]

The United States did not favor impunity for German war criminals. Instead, and in contrast to the enthusiasm for the potential of the Permanent Court of Arbitration, Washington was suspicious of super-national judicial organs. Relying on precedent, the secretary of state proposed a more conventional mechanism to prosecute the Germans: the United States, along with each of the aggrieved allies, would erect "a military tribunal within its own jurisdiction to pass upon violations of the laws and customs of war" for crimes against its citizens and property.[19] In its *Memorandum of Reservations*, the U.S. delegation reaffirmed that "those responsible for violations of the laws and customs of war should be punished for their crimes, moral and legal." However, in the end, the Americans were outvoted.[20] The commission, responding pragmatically to the fact that Germany had waged war on many countries, recommended a veritable revolution in international law: international courts, not domestic ones, would hold individual war criminals responsible for their transgressions.

Despite America's obstructionism on the commission, Washington had at times voiced support for the punishment of German war criminals. The First World War was a less costly and searing experience for the United States than for its European allies. In consequence, the Europeans pursued war crimes tribunals with much more determination. The German actions that left American noncombatants dead, however—unlimited submarine warfare—did indeed arouse the United States to call for postwar punishment. After the May 1915 sinking of the *Lusitania*, which killed 128 American citizens, Washington warned Berlin that the United States would seek "strict accountability." Using the language of law, not just war, the secretary of state demanded that "the officer of the German Navy responsible for the sinking of the *Lusitania* . . . be punished for having committed a lawless and inhumane act in thus causing the death of citizens of the United States." In the aftermath of the *Lusitania*, President Woodrow Wilson even privately entertained the notion that this wanton violation of international law should be countered with international justice. The United States' declaration of war against Germany in April 1917 focused on the war crime of unlimited submarine warfare, condemning the Second Reich for discarding "all restraints of law or of humanity." Arriving in France in December 1918, the president again foretold "the certainty of just punishment" for war criminals.[21] While America was dubious at Paris of unprecedented multinational tribunals, it is relevant that the United States shared the same core legal objective as the Europeans: war criminals should not be immune from justice.

The United States did accommodate the Europeans' drive for postwar justice, but sought to make it less sweeping. Compromises among the peacemakers led to the passage of Articles 227 and 228 of the Versailles Treaty. Article 227 charged the Kaiser with "a supreme offense against international morality and the sanctity of treaties." The indictment was political and moral in nature—based on "international morality," not international law. Nonetheless, Article 227 was revolutionary in holding a head of state to account. (The trial of the Kaiser would never come to fruition: the Netherlands, where the German monarch fled after the war, refused to extradite the royal fugitive.)

Article 228 called upon Germany to extradite hundreds of war criminals for trial at the hands of the Allies. To ameliorate the fear that the trials would further destabilize Germany, the Allies were later reluctantly pressured into allowing the German Supreme Court to try these individuals instead. The trials at Leipzig devolved into a farce. Only a dozen accused criminals were eventually tried. Those convicted received light jail sentences.[22] The Leipzig experience was on one hand a cautionary tale about the political risk potentially posed by holding the perpetrators to account, and on the other a cautionary tale about the risk of impunity when the vanquished are responsible for assessing the wartime conduct of their own citizens. The inherent danger in "victors' justice" is vengefulness. The inherent danger of local justice is impunity. The desire for a procedure that mitigates these risks is the origin of the idea of international justice.

Despite episodic rumblings that the United States would seek justice against liable German submariners, the American delegation focused its energies on Wilson's Fourteen Points. Above all, Wilson aspired to capitalize on the historic global summit to further progressive principles and erect a new liberal international order in the hope of averting another European catastrophe. For the United States, war crimes tribunals were a secondary concern. The liberal tenets that Wilson laid out in his Fourteen Points— self-determination, democratic government, international law, and collective security—became hallmarks of twentieth-century international relations, contending for influence with the more "realist" school that sees great-power conflict as ameliorable, if at all, only by carefully maintaining a balance of power.[23] "More than any American administration before or since," political scientist Gary Bass has noted, "the Wilson administration based its vision of world order on international law."[24] Wilson tapped into the broader American tradition of desire for a rule-based world—to be sure, rules not imposed on Americans by others, but written by Americans. Wilson roundly rejected realpolitik and a balance-of-power calculus. He envisioned a "community of power" that would promote law and justice. Wilson deemed the enterprise to try the Kaiser too punitive and retroactive: the introduction of collective security was instead forward-looking.[25] Both the Americans and the Europeans worked to advance liberal ends, but differed on the means (not for the last time). And of course the Second World War was a stark reminder of the limits of idealism, the ongoing relevance of power, and the danger of neglecting serious threats to international peace.

NUREMBERG AND TOKYO

The crimes the Nazi regime committed during the Second World War inspired a renewed, ultimately successful, effort to bring liable parties to justice in front of an international tribunal. Genuine planning to hold the German leadership accountable did not commence until the waning days of the war. In November 1943, the Moscow Declaration, signed by President Franklin Roosevelt, Soviet ruler Joseph Stalin, and British prime minister Winston Churchill, proclaimed that Germans responsible for "atrocities, massacres and executions" would be punished according to the laws of the aggrieved nations. The declaration assured that the Germans would be "judged on the spot by the peoples whom they outraged." The declaration offered local judgment for those Germans who had committed atrocities in particular places—that is, Czech judgment for those who killed

Czechs—but reserved for later the fate of major war criminals whose crimes had no geographic localization, like Adolf Hitler and Hermann Göring. Amid the passions of the war, it seemed that mass executions, not trials, would be the fate of accused war criminals. At the Tehran Conference that year, Stalin was publicly talking about executing 50,000 Germans.[26] Churchill was considering executing 50–100 top Axis criminals. However, the lobbying of Secretary of War Henry Stimson—with the strong support of the U.S. military, including Army Chief of Staff General George Marshall—convinced Roosevelt to pursue judicial means to punish offenders.

With the urging of Stimson, the president disavowed Treasury Secretary Henry Morgenthau's plan to demilitarize and partition postwar Germany and summarily execute its leadership. The stark philosophical differences between Stimson and Morgenthau boiled over into an intense White House debate in late 1944. In making his case against the Morgenthau Plan, Stimson enlisted Supreme Court Justice Felix Frankfurter, who agreed with him that the United States "must give [the Nazis] the substance of a fair trial and that they cannot be railroaded to their death without trial." Stimson felt that Soviet-style executions were beneath the United States' standards: "There would be methods used . . . in the liquidation of the military clique in Germany which the United States would not like to participate in directly." A lawyer by training, the secretary of war wanted American legal precepts to guide the Allied treatment of the Nazis. Stimson insisted that the Nazis be afforded such basic protections as notification of charges, the right of self-defense, and the ability to summon witnesses. Emboldened by the blessing of Frankfurter, Stimson wanted the international tribunal to meet the basic standards of the Bill of Rights.[27]

Roosevelt approved the War Department's plan for war crimes trials in January 1945. He wrote at the time: "The charges against the top Nazis should include an indictment for waging aggressive warfare, in violation of the Kellogg Pact."[28] The judicial scheme became official Allied policy with the February 1945 Yalta Memorandum: "Condemnation of these criminals after a trial, moreover, would command maximum public support in our own times and receive the respect of history." Although British and American public opinion would have likely supported summary execution of Axis war criminals at least initially, elite opinion recognized that an important international norm was shifting. The Allies appreciated that history, in light of the advances in the laws of war, would disapprove of the summary executions of Germans without trials.[29]

"At the end of America's most brutal war ever, the Germans would be accorded the benefit of legal procedure as it had evolved in America, because of an American belief in the rightness of its own domestic legalism," Bass concludes. He emphasizes the leadership the United States offered in bringing the Nuremberg tribunals to reality.[30] The United States took the dramatic step of seconding U.S. Supreme Court Justice Robert Jackson to serve as the chief prosecutor at Nuremberg. He was a true believer in the international tribunal's promise that the force of law would come to replace the force of arms.[31] Twenty-four Nazis were indicted, twenty-two were prosecuted, and in the end, twelve were sentenced to death.[32] The enduring and prodigious legacy of Nuremberg was the expansion of the reach of international law by holding senior officials personally accountable in a multinational setting for their war crimes.

While orchestrating the trial of Nazi war criminals in Europe, the United States also led the effort to hold Japanese war criminals to account. U.S. General Douglas MacArthur, the Supreme Commander for the Allied Powers in the Pacific, enjoyed the most influential role in steering the efforts to punish the Japanese. The international lawyer M. Cherif Bassiouni has commented, "Virtually every aspect of justice in the Far East was guided by MacArthur's views and his political perspectives on the region."[33] MacArthur decreed the establishment of the International Military Tribunal for the Far East in January 1946. The United States led the investigation of war crimes and drew up the rosters of the accused Japanese.

The procedure was fraught, however, with political considerations and a sense of arbitrariness. The "American Caesar," not the chief prosecutor, rendered the most significant decision of the whole endeavor: to grant Japanese Emperor Hirohito immunity. To several Americans, the United States' pragmatic and overriding concerns about ensuring a smooth occupation of Japan tarnished the legal integrity of the project. A senior American military intelligence officer blasted the proceedings as the "worst hypocrisy in recorded history."[34] To others, MacArthur's perspective on the need to strike a balance between competing goods was the correct course. Sitting in Tokyo from May 1946 to November 1948, the tribunal, which consisted of eleven judges from various nations, tried twenty-five senior military and political authorities for war crimes. Though the tribunal handed down stringent punishments, over the ensuing years, the Americans utilized their authority to grant clemency and shorten the prison sentences of convicted war criminals.[35] While the United States strove to punish those responsible, the realities of the occupation shaped the Tokyo tribunal.[36]

Of course neither the European nor the Pacific judicial procedures contemplated investigating the actions of the victors in winning the war, from Dresden to Tokyo to Hiroshima and

Nagasaki—any more than William Tecumseh Sherman's "hard war" March to the Sea in 1864 was subjected to legal scrutiny.

American Advocacy in the Early Efforts to Form an ICC

In the wake of the World War II international tribunals, the newly formed United Nations General Assembly, at the request of the United States, in 1946 affirmed the broad principles of Nuremberg. The principles Stimson and Jackson passionately championed—the universal accountability of individuals for war crimes and aggression—began to take root in the theory if not the practice of international law.

The idea for the creation of a permanent international criminal court gained momentum in the United Nations in the optimistic postwar environment of international cooperation. In 1948 the United States lobbied for the inclusion of language in the Genocide Convention that would call for the establishment of such a court. The American representative on the presiding committee noted that "it was precisely because it had been felt that national courts might not be sufficiently effective in the punishment of genocide that States had realized the need for an international convention on the subject."[37] This statement underscores the evolution in U.S. policy toward international justice that had unfolded over the decades. Three decades earlier, the American delegation at Versailles was advocating the use of domestic courts to try German war criminals. In response to American pressure in the 1940s, in the text of the resolution passing the Genocide Convention, the General Assembly instructed its International Law Commission to study "the desirability and possibility of establishing an international judicial organ for the trial of persons charged with genocide or other crimes over which jurisdiction will be conferred upon that organ by international conventions."[38]

Subsequently, in 1951, the Special Committee of the General Assembly drafted a working statute for the creation of the court. Two years later, another UN committee revised the existing plan to accommodate the reservations of member states. This 1953 blueprint outlined an envisioned court that would receive jurisdiction through convention, special agreement, or unilateral decision; while it would not provide for trial by jury, the court would guarantee defendants many of the rights enshrined in the U.S. Constitution.[39]

Then, because of strong opposition from the United Kingdom, American enthusiasm for the court waned. A U.S. diplomat assigned to the negotiations insisted that, while Washington remained open to the project, the court should have jurisdiction only over those individuals whose states have become parties.[40] And the 1954 publication of a Draft Code of Offenses against the Peace and Security of Mankind, listing thirteen indictable international crimes, became a stumbling block in the establishment of the judicial organ. The states responsible for the draft could not agree on the definition of "aggression."[41] Since the prosecution of bellicose leaders who waged expansionist wars would be one of the central duties of the court, there was little reason to further contemplate the venture until consensus was reached.

The cold war standoff between the two superpowers frustrated any meaningful progress on the issue. The Soviet Union, with veto power in the Security Council, interpreted the proposed court as an infringement on its sovereignty and became a stalwart opponent.[42] Although the UN General Assembly passed a nonbinding resolution defining aggression in 1974, the language has been subject to sharp criticism ever since, and negotiators of the Rome

Statute themselves were unable to come to agreement, putting the question off to deliberations that are now under way. Plans for an international criminal court continued to flounder in the contentious atmosphere of cold war politics.[43]

AMERICA'S ROLE IN THE MODERN MOVEMENT TO FORM AN ICC

The reshaping of the geopolitical landscape in the waning years of the cold war generated a new opening for pursuit of an international criminal court. The difficulty that states encountered in prosecuting two mounting transnational crimes—terrorism and drug trafficking—spurred the international community to seek a global forum to more effectively address the two concerns. As such, the intended purview of the court pivoted away from war crimes and genocide toward terrorism and narcotics. National pride and concerns about sovereignty rendered many governments reluctant to extradite their own citizens to foreign judicial bodies. Other states had scant interest in prosecuting suspects at all or simply lacked the witnesses and evidence to do so. The unwillingness of Libya to extradite to the United States Libyan citizens accused of orchestrating the 1988 terrorist bombing of Pan Am flight 103 exemplified the growing international conundrum. The idea began to take hold that a "neutral" judicial forum might make it easier for states like Libya to be more cooperative. States harboring suspects would be more inclined, in this view, to extradite suspects to an international court. In the absence of such judicial machinery, states resorted to ad hoc measures, such as sanctions in the case of the United States and Libya, to enforce the law.[44] By the 1990s, the existing international criminal law system had revealed plenty of shortcomings. Traditional concepts of sovereignty, jurisdiction, and state responsibility were evolving in response to transnational threats. Many had come to believe that a permanent, formal, and legitimate judicial mechanism was required to prosecute such elusive criminals, though concerns about sovereign rights remained.

American support in both governmental and nongovernmental circles emerged amid this renewed campaign for an international criminal court. The American Bar Association as early as 1978 urged the State Department to start negotiations to create a court to try cross-border crimes of hijacking and violence against diplomats. (The ABA would reinforce its advocacy in 1990 and again in 1992.)[45] The U.S. Congress's enactment of the Omnibus Diplomatic Security and Anti-Terrorist Act of 1986 broadened U.S. jurisdiction to include foreign nationals who committed crimes that injured American citizens. This legislation codified the United States' commitment to bring certain violent criminals to justice irrespective of political boundaries. Reflecting the consensus of the American legal community, in 1987 the Restatement (Third) of the Foreign Relations Law of the United States affirmed U.S. jurisdiction over "conduct outside . . . [U.S.] territory that has or is intended to have substantial effect within its country."[46] The next step in this evolutionary process targeted transnational fugitives: the 1988 Anti-Drug Abuse Act expressed the interest of Congress in an international criminal court designed to prosecute drug traffickers.[47] The U.S. House of Representatives, in a nonbinding resolution, broadened this appeal the following year: "[The United States] should pursue the establishment of an International Criminal Court to assist the international community in dealing more effectively with those acts of terrorism, drug trafficking, genocide and torture."[48] Through these legislative acts and resolutions, the United States codified and promoted the view that international criminals should not be allowed to hide behind state sovereignty and remain immune to accountability. The 101st Congress in October 1990 enacted H.R. 5114, recommending that the president explore the creation of an international criminal court in hopes of more effectively combating egregious transnational crimes.[49]

The push in the Democratic-majority Congress for the court was met with cautious pessimism in the Republican White House of Ronald Reagan and George H. W. Bush. However, Iraqi dictator Saddam Hussein's invasion and war crimes against Kuwait in the Persian Gulf War heralded a reinvigorated spirit of international unity and judicial accountability. That the UN Security Council was able to rally together for the first time to act collectively and repulse an act of aggression fostered this attitudinal shift. The Executive Branch began to share some of Congress's enthusiasm for an international criminal court. Both Secretary of State James Baker and Undersecretary of State Robert Kimmitt told Congress in September 1990 that the court deserved serious consideration from the White House.[50] Nevertheless, the White House was still wary. The American stance in the following years at the Sixth Committee of the UN International Law Committee's negotiations over the court remained "ambivalent, if not negative."[51]

The Democratic Congress continued to vocalize its support for a court. Senate Joint Resolution 32 of 1993—dubbed the International Criminal Court Act—called "for the United States to support efforts of the United Nations to conclude an international agreement to establish an international criminal court." The text of the resolution noted that the judicial body would "serve the interests of the United States and the world community" and that "the United States delegation should make every effort to advance this proposal at the United Nations." According to the legislation, the freedom and security of the international community depended on institutionalizing the rule of law at the global level. The Senate specifically cited the legacy of the post–World War II tribunals as demonstrative that "fair and effective prosecution of war criminals could be carried out in an international forum."[52] Despite Washington's common reference to the spirit of Nuremberg, serious concerns about the court's jurisdiction and powers remained.

THE BALKAN AND RWANDA AD HOC TRIBUNALS

The atrocities of the wars in the former Yugoslavia in the 1990s and the 1994 genocide in Rwanda cried out for accountability. The conclusion of the cold war fostered a political climate favorable to such a goal for the first time in half a century. With the demise of the Soviet Union, the United States emerged as the dominant power on the Security Council. The Clinton administration used this unrivaled position to urge the establishment of the International Criminal Tribunal for the former Yugoslavia (ICTY) in 1993 and the International Criminal Tribunal for Rwanda (ICTR) in 1994, the first such tribunals since the Second World War. According to international lawyer John Cerone, "It is clear that without the support of the United Sates, the ICTs would never have come into being."[53] The State Department viewed the proceedings of the ICTR as imperative to the future of peace and stability in Central Africa.[54] In light of concentration camps being constructed once again in Europe, U.S. Permanent Representative to the UN Madeleine Albright drew on the tradition of American advocacy for international justice to promote ICTY: "The Nuremberg principles have been reaffirmed. The lesson that we are all accountable to international law may finally have taken hold in our collective memory."[55]

At the outset, it seemed that the tribunals were stillborn. The ICTY was underfunded. Disturbed by this development, Washington provided over $93 million to the ICTY. Financial and in-kind contributions aside, however, the American record is more ambiguous. For fear of casualties, the Clinton administration dragged its feet in dispatching soldiers to war-torn Bosnia. This unwillingness to deploy American forces to the Balkans undermined the capabilities of the ICTY prosecutor. For example, the State Department and the Pentagon—fearing Serb retaliation—declined in June 1993 to provide military engineers to aid with the forensic investigation of a mass grave in Croatia.[56] The United States and its NATO allies were reluctant to task NATO troops with arresting accused war criminals. It took some time to reorient the U.S. intelligence community toward the provision of useful intelligence to the ICTY prosecutor. This was due to many factors, including the collection of information from sources and methods that could not be disclosed, development of procedures for declassification of intelligence and acceptable protection of classified information, staff shortages to review the ICTY's requests for information, and the lack of specificity in many of the ICTY requests. Shortly after the Srebrenica genocide of July 1995, aerial imagery flowed more quickly to the ICTY. By 1998 the United States had become more active in seeking to arrest indicted war criminals and increasingly forthcoming with its own intelligence. The Kosovo conflict in 1999 accelerated the government's cooperation with the ICTY. The United States also exerted diplomatic and financial pressure on Serbia to arrest Ratko Mladic and Radovan Karadzic, the two most notorious fugitives.

THE SADDAM TRIAL

Human rights proponents long sought the punishment of Saddam Hussein for crimes committed during his brutal years as president of Iraq. Following the 1990 invasion of Kuwait, government officials also raised the possibility of a trial for war crimes, including both British Prime Minister Margaret Thatcher and President George H. W. Bush.[57] The European Commission drafted a letter to the UN secretary-general requesting that he examine trying Saddam for violations of the Genocide Convention after Saddam's suppression of the Kurdish revolt that followed his ejection from Kuwait by U.S.-led forces. Saddam remained firmly in power, however, despite his defeat in 1991, a fact that reflected the Bush administration's limited objectives for the first Gulf War. The Clinton administration explored several avenues to investigate and issue indictments against Saddam and his regime, including creation of an ad hoc international criminal tribunal by the Security Council similar to ICTY and ICTR, but these efforts met firm opposition from some Security Council members. It was not until the 2003 invasion of Iraq and subsequent capture of Saddam that the former Iraqi leader would be put on trial, in a "hybrid" process that was widely criticized for a lack of due process, secrecy, a rush to mete out punishment, and a botched and controversial execution.

After Saddam's capture, many sought his trial before an international tribunal or hybrid court. The rift in the Security Council over the Iraq invasion, however, worked against efforts to mount an international trial. Countries opposing the war feared an international tribunal would confer legitimacy on the invasion after the fact. European opposition to capital punishment magnified differences with the Americans and Iraqis.[58] Bringing Saddam before the International Criminal Court was never a serious option. It would have required Security Council referral, a course the United States, which still actively opposed the Court, sought to avoid, and Saddam's worst crimes were outside the jurisdiction of the Court in any case, because they took place before the Court was established.

The head of the Coalition Provisional Authority, Paul Bremer, wielded veto power over decisions concerning the procedure and indictments. Critics condemned the trial for failing to meet international standards. In the end, Iraqis seeking to punish Saddam, while attempting to manifest their own sovereignty despite the American occupation, were permitted by the American-led occupation authorities to try Saddam essentially with limited outside input. The Court was staffed with Iraqi judges and Iraqi prosecutors only, with foreign experts in international law permitted to advise the court.[59]

The controversy that swirled around the flawed trial of Saddam served to weaken principles the United States had espoused in other conflicts. Perhaps the best that can be said is that having swung that far, the pendulum was poised to begin to swing back.

CHAPTER THREE

AMERICAN POLICY TOWARD THE ICC

From Antagonism to Acquiescence

THE UNITED STATES has had an ambivalent and tentative relationship with the International Criminal Court from the beginning. Although the United States supported the creation of a permanent international criminal tribunal early on, this support waned as negotiations toward a concrete institution progressed.[1] During the Clinton administration, official policy eventually settled on a formal but weak mandate to seek the establishment of a permanent international court. President Clinton expressed this desire repeatedly, most notably in a speech before the UN General Assembly in September 1997. "The United Nations must be prepared to respond, not only by setting standards," he said, "but by implementing them."[2] This signal of American support helped reinvigorate negotiations toward the Court's creation.

The history of those negotiations has been examined exhaustively elsewhere.[3] But it is important to note here that the results of the Rome Conference diverged from American interests at least in part because the U.S. government was internally divided. At the time, the reality of a Democratic White House at loggerheads with a Republican Congress, and turf battles between the State Department and the Pentagon, ensured that no matter how hard American negotiators in Rome tried, their proposals often came late in the game and, as a result, failed to gain traction or were easily displaced by carefully crafted proposals from coalitions with different agendas. These shifting coalitions—at various times comprising smaller or developing states, nonaligned states, and even U.S. allies—found success on a number of critical issues: The independence of the prosecutor and the inclusion of the crime of aggression within the Court's mandate are two issues over which like-minded nations skillfully outmaneuvered U.S. objections. As it became clear that the United States and its European allies were not necessarily on the same page, those countries wishing to isolate Washington seized the opportunity to do so.

As a result of these maneuvers, the Rome Statute contained provisions that the United States had strongly and vocally opposed during the negotiations, and the delegation voted against the treaty's text at the close of the Rome Conference. At the same time, U.S. negotiators did not leave Rome empty-handed. They secured several key provisions in the final text of the treaty, including adoption of the principle of "complementarity," more precise definitions of the Court's jurisdiction, the ability of the UN Security Council to intervene to defer cases, and the decision to postpone the definition of the crime of aggression, effectively removing the controversial crime from the books for a decade. Nor did the United States cease its engagement; over the next two years, U.S. diplomats continued to participate, and in some cases led in the drafting of supplemental court documents, including the elements of crimes and the rules of procedure and evidence.

Given this mixed result, President Clinton waited until the last possible day, December 31, 2000, to sign the Rome Statute. He did so with serious misgivings, acknowledging that there are "significant flaws in the treaty." Clinton specifically noted his concern that the Court would "not only exercise authority over personnel of states that have ratified the treaty, but also claim jurisdiction over personnel of states that have not." As a result, he did not refer the treaty to the Senate for advice and consent to ratification and recommended that his successor not do so "until our fundamental concerns are satisfied." Nonetheless, Clinton signed the treaty because, as he argued, doing so allowed the United States to remain "in a position to influence the evolution of the court." Because the United States has "a long history of commitment to the principle of accountability," working toward "a properly constituted and structured International Criminal Court would make a profound contribution in deterring egregious human rights abuses worldwide."[4]

In his statement, President Clinton's mention of "significant flaws" in the Rome Statute referred in particular to its purported jurisdiction over personnel in states that have not ratified the treaty. Independent critics of the Court have voiced six main objections to the treaty: (1) the Court's assertion of jurisdiction over some nationals of non-party states; (2) the prosecutor's ability to initiate cases on his own; (3) the lack of external oversight by or accountability to the international community; (4) deficiencies in the due process protections afforded to defendants; (5) and more technical problems, including the inability of states to lodge reservations with the treaty and defects in the "opt-out" provisions that offer states that are not party to the Rome Statute fewer protections than those that ratify it. In addition to these problems, which stem from the text of the treaty, some critics object to the

Court on more ideological grounds, citing it as (6) part of a growing international bureaucracy that erodes U.S. sovereignty and undermines U.S. freedom of action.[5]

Critics' Objections to the ICC

In the paragraphs that follow we spell out in greater detail as faithfully as possible the objections of critics. It should be noted that supporters of the Court have proffered rebuttals to these criticisms from the time they were first advanced. We do not summarize those rebuttals here. We address critics' concerns in the following chapters, especially in light of the Court's record of performance since its inception in 2002.

Jurisdiction over Nationals of States That Are Not Members of the Court

The most prominent objection to the Rome Statute concerns a provision in Article 12 permitting the Court to exercise jurisdiction over non-party nationals when crimes are committed on the territory of a State Party (the term used in official documents to refer to states that have ratified the treaty). Specifically, the Court has jurisdiction where "the State on the territory of which the conduct in question occurred" has ratified the Rome Statute. Although this provision led many to fear that the Court would prosecute American peacekeepers operating abroad, critics' concerns are broader: assertion of jurisdiction over non-party nationals violates the international norm that treaties bind only those nations that ratify them.[6] As a result, the Rome Statute is seen by critics to erode nations' sovereign right to choose what agreements, if any, they make with other nations.

Prosecutorial Independence

Many critics also protested and continue to object to the prosecutor's ability under the Rome Statute to initiate cases on his or her own, a process that requires the consent of two of three judges in a Pre-Trial Chamber. The *proprio motu*—self-initiating prosecutor—power in Article 15 permits the prosecutor to "initiate investigations . . . on the basis of information on crimes within the jurisdiction of the Court" and, if "there is a reasonable basis to proceed with an investigation," to submit information to the Pre-Trial Chamber to authorize such an investigation. In other words, if the prosecutor learns of crimes within the Court's jurisdiction, he or she can initiate an investigation (with judicial consent) without the approval of any State Party or any international body, such as the UN Security Council. To many critics, this power evokes fear that a malevolent prosecutor could initiate cases to pursue political ends. Others note that the prosecutor's ability to act on any "information on crimes" risks overwhelming the Court with frivolous complaints and baseless accusations, and the very nature of the *proprio motu* power would unnecessarily embroil the prosecutor in controversy and force him to consider political factors in his decisionmaking.

Lack of Oversight and Accountability

Compounding these problems for opponents of the Court is the lack of external oversight or mechanisms to hold the Court accountable to the international community. For example, as Article 1 makes clear, the Court was created as an independent body "governed by the provisions of [the Rome] Statute," rather than subject to decisions of any other institution, such as the UN. This independence remains controversial. Unlike the Court, the international criminal tribunals that investigated crimes in

Rwanda and the former Yugoslavia were created only after the UN Security Council authorized them. The United States proposed a similar model of jurisdiction for the Court, arguing that it should have jurisdiction only over cases referred to it by the UN Security Council. Article 13(b) vests the Court with jurisdiction over cases referred by the Security Council, but the Rome Statute does not stop there; the Court can exercise its jurisdiction without Security Council involvement. This is not to say that the United Nations has no role: Article 16 permits the Security Council, by means of a Chapter VII resolution, to defer investigations or prosecutions by the Court for a period of twelve months. But such a resolution would be subject to veto by any of the Security Council's five permanent members. If the Court had been established such that it could take jurisdiction only pursuant to a Security Council referral, any veto power could derail a Court investigation; under Article 13(b), all five permanent members would have to agree to defer an investigation or prosecution for the one-year period. Critics feared that, without needing international approval to proceed, the Court might take on frivolous cases for improper purposes, which would in turn face a high hurdle for deferral in the Security Council.

Critics highlight similar problems with the "complementarity" regime, which is designed to ensure that the Court takes cases only when nations are "unwilling or unable genuinely to carry out the investigation or prosecution" (17[1]a). The issue is that, under the Rome Statute, it is the Court itself that decides whether a country's prosecution or investigation is adequate and genuine. In other words, a nation that disputes the Court's assertion of jurisdiction on the ground that it wants to deal with the crimes domestically has no place to turn. The Court's judges get the final say on these matters, which strikes some as a substantial infringement of sovereignty. This concern is amplified by more general complaints that the Court's bureaucracy—in all its branches—is functionally immune to oversight; few procedures are available for individual State Parties to enforce checks and balances on the Court's operations.

Politically Motivated Prosecutions

Underlying the three categories of objections above are the dual concerns that the Court could pursue politically motivated prosecutions of American troops or prominent U.S. officials and that, because the United States plays a unique role as a global superpower, unique protections for our military are necessary. For example, because Article 12 permits the Court to prosecute nationals of countries that have not ratified the Rome Statute for crimes committed on the territory of a State Party, American troops could be subject to prosecution by the Court while operating in a state that had ratified the treaty. This causes concern for many critics, particularly because the U.S. military is active globally.

The Court, critics fear, is open to manipulation by anti-American politicians. Opponents of the Court are concerned that anti-American nations might refer U.S. troops or officials for prosecution to discredit the United States in the international community. The lack of a U.S. veto over which cases the Court pursues leaves U.S. troops theoretically vulnerable to prosecution.

Protections for Defendants

Other criticisms of the Court are more specific to its procedures. Although the Rome Statute includes many provisions to protect the rights of the accused, it does not provide mirror equivalents to those in the U.S. Constitution. Opponents of the Court in the United States find these shortcomings unacceptable. Most notably, Article

67 does not provide for a trial by jury, nor does Article 74 require unanimity for a finding of guilt—two requirements at the core of the U.S. criminal justice system. There are also concerns about the scope of a defendant's confrontation rights and the potential for disputes to arise over assertions of double jeopardy, which is governed by Article 20. These issues are important but narrow. Some scholars raise the broader constitutional objection that ratification of the Rome Statute by the United States would violate Article III, Section 1, of the Constitution by improperly establishing a non–Article III tribunal. These critics contend that, no matter what protections the Court may provide, the Constitution prohibits transferring defendants to a court like the ICC.

Prohibition on Reservations and "Opt-out" Provisions That Give Nonparticipating States Few Protections

The treaty's text also gives rise to three technical objections. First, Article 120 of the Rome Statute prohibits reservations, which is a method countries commonly use to note their disagreement with discrete parts of a treaty; for instance, a nation might sign a treaty but craft a reservation that exempts it from one specific requirement. By disallowing reservations, the framers of the Rome Statute sought to establish ratification as an all-or-nothing proposition, placing the burden on countries to make their laws conform to the treaty rather than the other way around. Because some of the requirements placed on State Parties for cooperation with the Court could be construed to conflict with U.S. laws, critics contend that the United States could join the Court only with reservations on these matters. Without that option, they believe, the United States cannot become a State Party. Second, Article 124 of the Rome Statute permits State Parties but not other nations to opt out of jurisdiction for war crimes during the first seven years of the

Court's operation. Negotiators intended this provision to allow reluctant countries to become State Parties but observe the Court's progress before subjecting their citizens to jurisdiction. Oddly, or mistakenly, the provision does not give other countries the same ability. In other words, Article 124 creates the paradox of allowing the Court's members to be immune from prosecution while nations that did not ratify the treaty are not. Third, this problem arises again in Article 121, which governs new or amended crimes. Here, a State Party can exempt itself from new crimes that are added to the Court later, but countries that have not joined the Court cannot. Again, in these narrow scenarios, countries that have not signed the Rome Statute are actually more vulnerable to prosecution by the Court. Critics find these provisions unfair because they violate the norm of international treaty law that countries are bound only by what they agree to do.

Ideological Concerns

In addition to these problems, which stem from the final form of the Rome Statute, some critics object to the Court on more ideological grounds, citing it as part of a growing international bureaucracy that erodes U.S. sovereignty and freedom of action. To these opponents of the Court, the Rome Statute represents "a product of fuzzy-minded romanticism . . . not just naïve, but dangerous."[7] In their view, the Court would erode U.S. sovereignty by "transfer[ing] ultimate judgment on American military measures from the U.S. government to an international prosecutor."[8] More generally, they argue that formation of the Court would create another large international bureaucracy that would not be accountable to anyone, particularly not to American citizens. Critics also note that there is the potential for the Court to usurp the role of the UN Security Council, where the United States has veto power. According to this argument, before the Court's creation, the Security Council was the principal arbiter of disputes over international aggression or whether a nation's actions so violated international law as to allow other nations to compromise its sovereignty—either by military force or interference in domestic matters.[9] The Court would play a similar role, critics fear, sitting in judgment of the affairs of sovereign states. In doing so, the Court could undermine U.S. interests.

Efforts to Limit the Court

The administration of George W. Bush assumed power twenty days after Clinton affixed his signature to the Rome Statute and entered office broadly skeptical of international agreements, including the Rome Statute creating the International Criminal Court.[10] In the late 1990s and early 2000s, the Court became a rallying issue among conservatives, many of whom had access to or assumed positions in the new administration. They also had ardent supporters in Congress. Senator Rod Grams, for example, said the ICC was "a monster that must be slain," and Senator Jesse Helms, then chairman of the Senate Foreign Relations Committee, declared of President Clinton's eleventh-hour signing of the Rome Statute: "This decision will not stand."[11]

The new administration and Congress joined in a concerted diplomatic and legislative effort to discredit and undermine the Court. The administration took the unprecedented step of unsigning the treaty, entered into negotiations with over 100 countries to inoculate the United States from its provisions, sought and passed legislation to impose penalties on parties to the treaty who did not offer special protections to Washington, and required the Security Council to extend special protection to U.S. service members or risk a U.S. veto of peacekeeping and related military operations.

Over time, however, the Bush administration eased, or in most cases entirely eliminated these provisions under pressure from senior military leaders and the secretary of state, who complained about the harmful effects of the prohibitions on national security. In the meantime, domestic pressure groups, including evangelical groups with close ties to the White House as well as progressive groups, mounted effective public campaigns to urge action to prevent a second genocidal wave in Darfur. Dismay over the continuing conflict in Darfur, which the Bush administration correctly described as a genocide, forged a U-turn in the administration's policy toward the Court in its final years in office.

"Unsigning"

The most conspicuous step the Bush administration took to distance the United States from the ICC was a three-sentence letter sent in May 2002 to UN Secretary-General Kofi Annan by Under Secretary of State for Arms Control and International Security John Bolton, a longtime opponent of the ICC. Bolton's letter informed Secretary-General Annan that the United States no longer intended to become a party to the treaty and, accordingly, "the United States has no legal obligations arising from its signature on December 31, 2000."[12]

We believe that the legal impact of Bolton's letter was and remains minimal, though this point is debated in legal circles.[13] Whatever its legal significance, however, the political significance of the decision to "unsign" the treaty is not in dispute.

STATEMENTS ON U.S. POLICY TOWARD THE COURT

Secretary of State Hillary Rodham Clinton, written response to questions submitted during her confirmation hearing, January 2009
Without prejudging the outcome of the ICC prosecutor's recommendation to indict President Bashir, the President-Elect believes, as do I, that we should support the ICC's investigations, including its pursuit of perpetrators of genocide in Darfur. The Bush administration has indicated publicly a willingness to cooperate with the ICC in the Darfur investigation. I commend them for this position, which we also support. We can provide assistance in the investigation; we can and should work with our allies in this effort. This is important because it would send a sign of seriousness about Darfur and our determination to end the killings and bring those responsible for war crimes to justice.

U.S. Permanent Representative to the UN Susan Rice, Statement to the Security Council, January 29, 2009
The ad hoc war crimes tribunals for the Former Yugoslavia and Rwanda, and the hybrid tribunals in Sierra Leone and Cambodia, are actively prosecuting crimes involving violations of international humanitarian law. The International Criminal Court, which has started its first trial this week, looks to become an important and credible instrument for trying to hold accountable the senior leadership responsible for atrocities committed in the Congo, Uganda, and Darfur.

U.S. Permanent Representative to the UN Susan Rice, quoted in the Washington Post, *February 9, 2009*
It is our view that we support the ICC investigation and the prosecution of war crimes in Sudan, and we see no reason for an Article 16 deferral.

Senator Barack Obama, Presidential Campaign Questionnaire Response, October 6, 2007

Now that it is operational, we are learning more and more about how the ICC functions. The Court has pursued charges only in cases of the most serious and systemic crimes and it is in America's interests that these most heinous of criminals, like the perpetrators of the genocide in Darfur, are held accountable. These actions are a credit to the cause of justice and deserve full American support and cooperation. Yet the Court is still young, many questions remain unanswered about the ultimate scope of its activities, and it is premature to commit the U.S. to any course of action at this time. The United States has more troops deployed overseas than any other nation and those forces are bearing a disproportionate share of the burden in protecting Americans and preserving international security. Maximum protection for our servicemen and women should come with that increased exposure. Therefore, I will consult thoroughly with our military commanders and also examine the track record of the Court before reaching a decision on whether the U.S. should become a State Party to the ICC. My administration would continue to cooperate with ongoing ICC investigations in Sudan.

Senators John McCain and Bob Dole, Washington Post, *September 8, 2006*

We should publicly remind Khartoum that the International Criminal Court has jurisdiction to prosecute war crimes in Darfur and that Sudanese leaders will be held personally accountable for attacks on civilians.

Action at the Security Council

The Bush administration took an active role at the UN Security Council that further demonstrated its opposition to Rome Statute provisions. In more than one case, the administration put UN peacekeeping and other missions it backed at risk unless U.S. concerns about the reach of the ICC were specifically addressed in Security Council resolutions.

In the spring and summer of 2002, for example, the United States threatened to oppose resolutions extending UN-led or -authorized missions in East Timor, Croatia, and the Balkans unless the Security Council expressly granted in resolutions blanket immunity from the International Criminal Court for U.S. personnel. At the time, the United States had 700 blue-hatted peacekeepers in Bosnia and 8,000 troops serving in the UN-authorized NATO missions in Kosovo and Bosnia.[14]

On June 22, 2002, during proceedings on the usually routine renewal of the UN Mission in Bosnia and Herzegovina (UNMBH), the U.S. delegation agreed to extend the UN mandate for just nine days—until the day before the ICC was scheduled to enter into force. The United States agreed to extend the mandate further only after securing the inclusion of language that invoked Article 16 of the Rome Statute, ostensibly to give the United States and other non-party states blanket immunity from the Court for one year.[15]

American Service-Members' Protection Act

Before the 2002 entry into force of the Rome Statute, congressional opponents of the Court pursued a number of legislative responses, including preparing drafts of what would become the American Service-Members' Protection Act of 2002 (ASPA), signed into law by President Bush on August 2, 2002—one month after the ICC entered into force.[16] ASPA was sponsored and the effort was led in the Senate by the chairman of the Senate Foreign Relations Committee, Jesse Helms, and in the House by Majority Leader Tom DeLay. The Republican-led Congress managed to avoid a straight up or down vote by embedding the bill in a defense appropriations measure, which received bipartisan support on final passage.[17] Among the salient features of the act was the provision permitting the United States to use "all means necessary" to free a U.S. official from the Court's jurisdiction for any attempt to transfer him or her to the ICC. That provision earned the bill the nickname "The Hague Invasion Act," and not just among critics of the legislation. More central to ASPA 2002 was the requirement to suspend military aid to any country party to the ICC that did not enter into a bilateral immunity agreement (BIA) with the United States. BIAs, also known as bilateral nonsurrender agreements or Article 98 agreements, stipulated that the country will not transfer U.S. personnel—current or former government officials, military and otherwise—to the custody of the ICC.[18]

To enact these measures President Bush gave broad authority to John Bolton to conclude bilateral agreements. Between 2002 and 2007 the Office of Security Negotiations and Agreements in the State Department negotiated and secured Article 98 agreements from over 100 countries.[19] In the months immediately following the passage of ASPA, the European Union strongly urged the thirteen nations aspiring to join the EU to resist signing any immunity agreements with the United States for fear that .such agreements would undermine the nascent Court.[20] Nonetheless, pursuant to the act, President Bush announced on July 1, 2003, the suspension of military aid to thirty-five State Parties to the Court that had not entered into a bilateral agreement with the United States.

Over the next three years, twelve Latin American countries (including Brazil, Bolivia, Ecuador, and Mexico) lost funding totaling over $10 million. In 2005, Mercosur, the South American regional trade organization, issued a joint presidential declaration opposing U.S. BIA policy.[21]

In 2005 the administration increased the penalties for BIA non-compliance. The Nethercutt Amendment of 2005 was included in the FY2006 Consolidated Appropriations Act and broadened the ASPA penalties to also include prohibitions on economic aid provided under the Economic Support Funds (ESF) program.

REASSESSMENT

By 2005 the Bush administration's uncompromising stance began to weaken. The consequences of unilateralist policies, the positive track record of the Court, and recognition of the Court's utility—especially in dealing with situations like Darfur—fostered a period of reassessment. In addition, the new legal adviser at the State Department, John Bellinger III, wrote a transition paper expressing concern that the administration's position and tone toward the ICC was hurting America's reputation and urged that the administration try to change global perceptions during its second term.[22] Bellinger also gave a series of public speeches in which he said the United States would be willing to help the ICC's investigations, particularly the prosecutor's efforts in Sudan.

Without embracing the Court, many within the government began to reevaluate the costs of pursuing strident anti-ICC policies, a trend reinforced by the departure of some of the administration's most ardent ICC opponents. Newly appointed secretary of state Condoleezza Rice commented that blocking military assistance to nations seeking to combat terrorism was "sort of the same as shooting ourselves in the foot";[23] U.S. Southern Command officials asserted that ASPA restrictions were producing "unintended consequences," including significantly obstructing military modernization projects and severing strategic relationships with future military and civilian leaders;[24] and the Pentagon published a strategic report calling on Congress to consider removing military funding restrictions from ASPA.[25]

Responding to the pressure, the administration began scaling back anti-ICC legislation. In October 2006, President Bush signed an amendment to ASPA removing International Military and Education Training (IMET) restrictions from all nations.[26] A year and a half later Bush sought further amendments to ASPA to eliminate all Foreign Military Financing (FMF) restrictions on nations unwilling to enter Article 98 agreements with the United States, and stipulated that U.S. cooperation with the Court was now subject to the Dodd Amendment, which authorized the government to participate in a wide range of international justice efforts.[27] Combined, these two provisions defanged ASPA. In a final stroke, four days before leaving office, President Bush directed the secretary of state to waive the Nethercutt restrictions on sixteen nations. The Nethercutt Amendment has since expired and was not included in the 2009 appropriations omnibus bill.[28] In effect, the great tide of Bush's anti-ICC legislation had receded by the time President Obama took office.

The major turning point in the U.S. position on the ICC arose from the continuing conflict and humanitarian crisis in Darfur. By March 2004, the UN resident and humanitarian coordinator for Sudan diagnosed the situation as the "world's greatest humanitarian crisis"[29] and later that year Secretary of State Colin Powell told the Senate Foreign Relations Committee that the killings in Darfur constituted "genocide."[30]

The domestic call for U.S. action in Darfur came from many quarters. Human rights and aid organizations, including the International Crisis Group, Human Rights First, and the multireligious Save Darfur Coalition, built a strong base of support through awareness campaigns and through prominent popular voices. Evangelical organizations such as Samaritan's Purse, run by the Reverend Billy Graham's son Franklin, had been active in Sudan for more than two decades providing humanitarian assistance to the Christian communities affected by the bloody North–South civil war. By the beginning of President Bush's second term, religious consortium groups like the World Evangelical Alliance and Evangelicals for Darfur had launched effective lobbying campaigns for stronger U.S. action in Sudan.[31] Among those calling for greater action was President Bush's former senior policy adviser Michael Gerson, one of *Time* magazine's "25 Most Influential Evangelicals in America."[32]

By 2005 it was clear that there was no political will in Washington or other capitals to take military action to stop the killing. The administration settled instead on a policy aimed at ratcheting up pressure on the government of Sudanese president Omar al-Bashir at the Security Council. The U.S. desire for stronger Security Council action on Darfur led the administration to drop its prior policy of hostility toward the ICC and its desire for a new special tribunal for Darfur and accept instead the referral of Darfur to the ICC.

In March 2005, Permanent Representative of France to the United Nations Jean-Marc de La Sablière orchestrated a compromise resolution with safeguards built in to meet U.S. concerns. Resolution 1593 would refer the Darfur situation to the International Criminal Court with the crucial caveat that the jurisdiction of the investigation would be limited to Sudanese nationals and exclude all foreign peacekeeping forces and all persons hailing from states that are not party to the Rome Statute.[33] The resolution also specified that none of the expenses incurred in connection with the referral, investigation, or prosecution would be borne by any non–State Parties to the Rome Statute. The resolution, in effect, contained the protections that the United States had previously sought, while at the same time steering clear of possible conflict with the American Service-Members' Protection Act.[34]

In a move that took many by surprise, the United States abstained from the Security Council vote, thus signaling tacit approval, and Resolution 1593 passed. A senior administration official later said, "It's well known that we're not big supporters of the ICC, but the Court is the only game in town right now to bring accountability for the Darfur genocide, and we don't want to let Bashir off the hook quite so easily."[35]

In June 2005, ICC Prosecutor Luis Moreno-Ocampo announced that the prosecutor's office would open its investigation into the Darfur situation.[36] As the prosecutor began investigating President Bashir's inner circle, the Sudanese leader responded by pushing back against the Court. In April 2007, the ICC issued arrest warrants for Ahmad Haroun, Sudan's minister of state for the interior, and government-allied militia leader Ali Kushayb on several dozen counts of crimes against humanity and war crimes.[37] In response, President Bashir promoted both men and launched a public relations campaign in Khartoum to discredit the Court, claiming the ICC was anti-Sudan and anti-African.[38]

In July 2008, Ocampo widened the case, presenting evidence against President Bashir on charges of genocide, crimes against humanity, and war crimes.[39] The request was reviewed by a panel of ICC judges, and though they rejected the genocide charge, a warrant based on the other counts was issued March

4, 2009, the first time the ICC has issued a warrant for a sitting head of state.

The case against Bashir stirred an international debate framed as "peace versus justice." In the wake of Ocampo's request for an arrest warrant for President Bashir, many international observers and organizations came out against the proposed prosecution, fearing that the proceedings could derail any hopes for a peace process.[40] Pressure began to mount on European governments to invoke Article 16 of the Rome Statute, under which the Security Council may postpone an ICC investigation or prosecution for one year, with the possibility of indefinite renewals. The idea was to give Bashir an incentive to pursue peace. After an initial dalliance with the idea of delaying Court action, the French presidency of the EU adopted a harder line. "If the Sudanese authorities totally change their policy," President Nicolas Sarkozy announced, "then France would not be against using Article 16."[41] For his part, President Bashir launched a concerted lobbying effort in pursuit of an Article 16 vote, successfully securing support from the African Union and the Arab League. The Chinese representative to the UN, Wang Guangya, signaled that China, too, might push for postponement: "The indictment of the Sudanese leader proposed by the Prosecutor of the International Criminal Court is an inappropriate decision taken at an inappropriate time. China supports the reasonable request by the African Union and other organizations for the Council to take early action to suspend the indictment of the Sudanese leader by the ICC, in accordance with the relevant provisions."[42]

The "reasonable request" of the African Union that the international community cautiously consider the risks of prosecuting Bashir made it into the text of UN Resolution 1828 to extend the mandate of the African Union–United Nations Mission in Darfur

(UNAMID).[43] The U.S. delegation, angered that some countries were attempting to undermine the ICC investigation and concerned about linking an extension of the peacekeeping mandate to the ICC issue, abstained from the vote.[44] Deputy Permanent Representative to the UN Alejandro D. Wolff explained the U.S. position in a written statement: the "language added to the resolution would send the wrong signal to Sudanese President Bashir and undermine efforts to bring him and others to justice."[45]

By the end of its second term, the Bush administration had come to recognize the utility of the Court in dealing with cases such as the state-led genocide in Darfur. Accordingly, the United States softened its approach to the Court, and Congress followed the Bush lead in going along with efforts to weaken the strictures of ASPA.

Efforts to Accommodate the Court

With Democrats in control of the White House and Congress after the 2008 elections, the issue is whether the Bush administration's acquiescence in a greater role for the Court will be transformed into an explicit and comprehensive policy of support. An early indication is the effort by Congress to inoculate U.S. personnel from the Court's jurisdiction by enacting legislation to close any procedural gaps, real or perceived, between U.S. law and the crimes within the jurisdiction of the ICC.[46] The United States would then have further enhanced its legal infrastructure to investigate and prosecute U.S. citizens who might commit such crimes, denying the admissibility of the case before the ICC under Article 17 of the Rome statute.

The Senate Judiciary Subcommittee on Human Rights and the Law, headed by Senator Richard Durbin (D-Ill.), successfully pressed to enact two laws that go directly to the issue of establishing clear U.S. instruments to prosecute war crimes: the Genocide Accountability Act (GAA), which amends the federal criminal code to allow the prosecution of acts constituting genocide, and the Child Soldiers Protection and Accountability Act (CSPA), which criminalizes the recruitment or deployment of child soldiers. The GAA addresses crimes of genocide covered in Article 6 of the Rome Statute, and the CSPA addresses Article 8 §2(b)(xxvi), which describes as a war crime "conscripting or enlisting children under the age of fifteen years into the national armed forces or using them to participate actively in hostilities."[47] A third bill, the Trafficking in Persons Accountability Act, has been approved by the Senate and passage in the House is anticipated. The bill is directly relevant to the crime against humanity of enslavement, filling another gap in U.S. law.[48]

The larger trend to end U.S. hostility toward the ICC seems to have support in the Obama administration.[49] As a candidate, Obama signaled his intent to cooperate with the Court in close consultation with the military. In her confirmation hearing, Secretary of State nominee Hillary Clinton pledged that "we will end hostility towards the ICC, and look for opportunities to encourage effective ICC action in ways that promote U.S. interests by bringing war criminals to justice."[50] The Obama administration's U.S. permanent representative to the UN, Susan Rice, has said that the Court "looks to become an important and credible instrument for trying to hold accountable the senior leadership responsible for atrocities committed in the Congo, Uganda, and Darfur."[51]

The Bush administration began its tenure as a zealous opponent of the ICC and ended up acquiescing in the Court's work. But without a clear statement of policy, uncertainty about U.S.

intentions abounded within our military and diplomatic corps and resonated abroad.

The Obama administration has sent positive signals about the Court. The evolution of the U.S. position through the Bush administration's two terms and into the present administration is at least partly due to the fact that many of the worst fears about the Court have not been realized—and in fact the Court has built a respectable reputation in a short time.

CHAPTER FOUR

THE ICC'S RECORD

SINCE ITS BIRTH in 2002 the International Criminal Court has won respect in fulfilling its mission to bring those responsible for the most heinous crimes to justice. Although the prosecutor's investigations have progressed fitfully, where the Court has acted it has generally garnered support. The Court's judges have protected the rights of defendants and worked to enhance the ability of states to bring perpetrators of mass atrocities to justice in their own countries without resort to the ICC. The Court has also demonstrated an intention to protect victims and provide them with a voice in proceedings. The Court has rejected numerous dubious requests to investigate allegations, most notably in the case of Iraq. On an institutional level, the Court is fully operational, and when it acts, it does so with substantial moral authority, despite criticism in sub-Saharan Africa and elsewhere that the Court is overly focused on the South.

Although many criticisms of the Court paint a rhetorical picture of an extremely strong institution with a potentially renegade prosecutor, the reality has been rather different. The Court is weaker and more dependent than most of its critics supposed and many of its supporters hoped. It cannot investigate or arrest without the effective cooperation of states. The Court's resources are limited and are subject to financial oversight by the Assembly of States Parties. The prosecutor's powers are subject to judicial checks; for example, a review panel rejected the prosecutor's recommendation to charge the president of Sudan with genocide while accepting other recommended charges. The Court's actions are subject to ongoing political and NGO scrutiny, some of which has been frankly critical. There are additional reporting requirements on the prosecutor, including reports to the UN Security Council.

The Court has come in for its share of criticism, controversy, and disappointments. Perhaps most serious is that the Court has been unable to secure the arrest of all the individuals it has charged. Under the ICC system, states bear the responsibility for executing ICC arrest warrants, and thus far just four of the twelve individuals charged by the Court have been arrested and transferred to its custody.

On balance, however, the Court's record belies many of the objections raised by its critics, and many of the concerns that most worried American critics have been allayed in practice, if not put to rest. The prosecutor has avoided politically motivated prosecutions, enhancing the office's professional standing. The Court has acted to protect defendants' rights, enhancing the credibility of the Court's procedures and decisions. The prosecutor has cultivated cordial relations with the United States despite the estrangement between the Court and Washington, and he has not hesitated to appoint talented and experienced Americans to serve in key posts at the Court.

Formal Investigations Undertaken

Since the Court's first prosecutor, Argentine lawyer Luis Moreno-Ocampo, took office in June of 2003, he has launched formal investigations into four "situations": northern Uganda, the Democratic Republic of Congo (DRC), Sudan, and the Central African Republic (CAR). He has sought and received arrest warrants in each situation, and four defendants have been arrested and transferred to the Court's custody. Judicial proceedings in these cases are under way: charges against Congolese warlords Thomas Lubanga Dyilo, Germain Katanga, and Mathieu Ngudjolo Chui have been confirmed by the judicial review panel. Charges against Jean-Pierre Bemba Gombo were confirmed in June 2009. Nine arrest warrants remain outstanding. Two of the charged individuals are believed dead, leaving seven fugitives at large. This includes the president of Sudan, three senior leaders of the Lord's Resistance Army (LRA) in northern Uganda, a government official and military commander in Sudan, and a fourth rebel leader in the DRC. In addition are the requested arrest warrants naming three rebel commanders in Darfur for war crimes. Because the prosecutor can request such warrants confidentially, the Court may have issued additional warrants that have not been made public. The prosecutor is conducting preliminary investigations (analysis to determine whether investigation is warranted) into serious crimes committed in at least a half-dozen countries.

Northern Uganda

The prosecutor launched his first investigation in July 2004, following a referral from the government of Uganda in December 2003. This effort focused on northern Uganda, specifically, the Lord's Resistance Army, a small guerrilla group notorious for its forced conscription of children, brutal assaults on civilians, and sexual enslavement of girls. Since the LRA's campaign against the Ugandan government began in 1986, the group has abducted at least 20,000 women and children, more than 12,000 people have died, and the violence has displaced almost 2 million civilians from their homes. The United States designated the LRA a terrorist organization in 2001.

In July 2005, after a year-long investigation by the prosecutor's office, the Court issued five arrest warrants. The targets of the warrants were LRA chief Joseph Kony; his deputy, Vincent Otti; and three other members of the group's command: Raska Lukwiya, Okot Odhiambo, and Dominic Ongwen. According to the prosecutor, Lukwiya "was responsible for some of the worst attacks committed by the LRA during the investigated period." Odhiambo "commanded the most violent of the four brigades of the LRA," and Ongwen led another particularly brutal brigade. The Court initially issued the warrants under seal, because of security concerns, but released them to the public three months later.

The warrants alleged that Kony and Otti led an armed militia that "has engaged in a cycle of violence and established a pattern of 'brutalization of civilians' by acts including murder, abduction, sexual enslavement, mutilation, as well as mass burnings of houses and looting of camp settlements." As part of this campaign, "civilians, including children, [were] forcibly 'recruited' as fighters, porters and sex slaves to serve the LRA and to contribute to attacks against the Ugandan army and civilian communities." In his filings to the Court, the prosecutor described the "civilians in Northern Uganda [as] living in a nightmare of brutality and violence for more than nineteen years."

None of the individuals charged in the Ugandan situation has been arrested, although two of the five are believed dead.

Lukwiya was killed by government troops in battle in August 2006. Otti was killed a year later by other LRA commanders, acting under Kony's orders, after an internal dispute over participation in peace talks. Media reports indicated that, shortly before the warrants were unsealed in 2005, Ongwen also had been killed in combat; Odhiambo reportedly met the same fate in April 2008. The prosecutor's team subsequently conducted DNA tests, however, and the results indicated that the body suspected to be Ongwen was not his; reports of Odhiambo's death were also confirmed to be false. Odhiambo, Ongwen, and Kony remain at large.

Democratic Republic of Congo

The prosecutor's second investigation concerns the Democratic Republic of Congo. The cases commenced so far involve crimes committed in the eastern region of Ituri. The Congolese government referred the situation to the Court in April 2004, and the prosecutor launched an investigation two months later. Between January 2002 and December 2003, fighting between the Congolese military and regional powers Rwanda and Uganda fueled the growth of violent militias, which in turn exacerbated underlying tensions between the Hema and Lendu ethnic groups, among others. The resulting conflict killed more than 8,000 civilians and displaced more than half a million people from their homes. In addition to civilian deaths and forced displacement, sexual violence and the use of child soldiers were constant features of the conflict.

In February 2006, after more than eighteen months of investigation, the Court issued its first arrest warrant in the Congo situation. It charged Thomas Lubanga Dyilo, leader of the Union of Congolese Patriots (UPC), with three separate war crimes: enlist-

Summary of Investigations and Prosecutions by the International Criminal Court, as of April 2009

Country involved	Public arrest warrants issued	Criminal charges	Status
Northern Uganda	Joseph Kony	12 counts of crimes against humanity and 21 counts of war crimes	Fugitive
Referred by Ugandan government, December 2003	Vincent Otti	11 counts of crimes against humanity and 21 counts of war crimes	Died in 2007
Investigation opened, July 2004	Raska Lukwiya	1 count of crimes against humanity (enslavement) and 3 counts of war crimes	Died on August 12, 2006
	Okot Odhiambo	2 counts of crimes against humanity and 8 counts of war crimes	Fugitive, rumored to have died in April 2008
	Dominic Ongwen	3 counts of crimes against humanity and 4 counts of war crimes	Fugitive
Democratic Republic of the Congo (DRC)	Thomas Lubanga Dyilo	Conscripting or enlisting child soldiers	Transferred to the ICC March 17, 2006; trial halted on June 13, 2008
Referred by the DRC government, March 2004	Germain Katanga	6 counts of war crimes and 3 counts of crimes against humanity, including murder, sexual slavery, and intentionally directing attacks at civilians	Transferred to the ICC October 17, 2007; confirmation of charges hearing completed
Investigation opened, July 2004	Mathieu Ngudjolo Chui	9 counts of war crimes and crimes against humanity, including murder, sexual slavery, inhumane treatment, the use of child soldiers in hostilities, and unlawful attacks against civilians	Transferred to the ICC February 6, 2008; confirmation of charges hearing completed
	Bosco Ntaganda	Enlisting and conscripting child soldiers	Fugitive

Country involved	Public arrest warrants issued	Criminal charges	Status
Central African Republic (CAR) Referred by CAR government, December 2004 Investigation opened, May 2007	Jean-Pierre Bemba Gombo	Crimes against humanity and war crimes, including rape and torture	Transferred to the ICC July 3, 2008; confirmation of charges hearing completed
Darfur, Sudan Referred by UN Security Council, March 2005 Investigation opened, June 2005	Ahmed Haroun	51 counts of war crimes and crimes against humanity, including murder, rape, torture, and persecution	Fugitive
	Ali Kushayb	51 counts of war crimes and crimes against humanity, including murder, rape, torture, and persecution	Fugitive
	Omar al-Bashir	7 counts of war crimes and crimes against humanity, including murder, extermination, and rape	Fugitive

ing children under the age of 15, conscripting children under the age of 15, and using children under the age of 15 to participate actively in hostilities. When the warrant was unsealed on March 17, 2006, Lubanga was already under detention in the DRC on unrelated charges. He was transferred to The Hague three days later, and the Court confirmed the charges after a three-week hearing in November. Trial was scheduled for June 2008 but was delayed to resolve defense concerns about access to exculpatory evidence. This dispute led the Trial Chamber to suspend Lubanga's trial indefinitely and order him released. The Appeals Chamber disagreed, however, and the issues were subsequently resolved. Lubanga's trial began in January 2009 and is continuing at this writing. The dispute on the Court over the issue of access to exculpatory evidence is an indication of the seriousness with which the Court takes defendants' rights.

Two other Congolese militia leaders are in custody at the Court: Germain Katanga, the leader of the Force de résistance patriotique en Ituri (FRPI), and Mathieu Ngudjolo Chui, a former leader of the National Integrationist Front (FNI) and a colonel in the Armed Forces of the DRC (FARDC). The prosecutor charged both men with nine counts of war crimes and crimes against humanity for their roles in an attack on the village of Bogoro, which resulted in the deaths of 200 civilians. The charges include murder or willful killing, inhumane acts, sexual slavery, rape, cruel or inhuman treatment, using children to participate actively in hostilities, outrages upon personal dignity, intentional attack against the civilian population, pillaging, and destruction of property. Although the Court issued both warrants in July 2007, they were not made public at the time. Charges against Katanga were announced on October 18, 2007, the day after he was transferred to the Court by the Congolese government. Ngudjolo Chui was arrested and transferred to the Court four months later, and the Court joined their cases for trial.

In the coming months, the prosecutor expects to initiate further investigations in the DRC, focusing specifically on the region of the Kivu provinces. He has also indicated that he "plans to bring a case against those who organized and financed militias active in the DRC." Such a case could include government officials in the DRC itself or in neighboring Uganda and Rwanda, two countries that played a major role in destabilizing the country.

As the prosecutor continues to consider charges in the Congo, at least one defendant remains at large. In April 2008, the Court unsealed an arrest warrant for Bosco Ntaganda, a former leader of the Forces patriotiques pour la libération du Congo (FPLC), and alleged current chief of the Congrès national pour la défense du peuple (CNDP). The prosecutor sought charges against Ntaganda at the same time that he applied for a warrant against Lubanga, and the two men face the same three charges related to the use of child soldiers, including enlisting children under the age of 15, conscripting children under the age of 15, and using children under the age of 15 to participate actively in hostilities. Ntaganda remains a fugitive.

Darfur, Sudan

The prosecutor's most prominent investigation began in 2005, after the UN Security Council voted to confer jurisdiction on the Court to investigate crimes in the Darfur region of Sudan.[1] The Security Council referral followed a report by the UN International Commission of Inquiry on Darfur, which determined that crimes against humanity and war crimes had occurred in the region and recommended that the Security Council refer the situation to the Court pursuant to Article 13(b) of the Rome Statute.

The council did so on March 31, 2005, in Resolution 1593. The vote on the measure was eleven in favor and none against, with four countries abstaining, including two veto holders, the United States and China.

The conflict in Darfur began in 2003. Local rebel groups took up arms against the government, accusing Khartoum of neglecting the region and favoring certain ethnic factions over others; disputes over land and access to natural resources became violent. The Sudanese government responded to the insurgency by bombing villages from the air and supporting Janjaweed militias, composed of members of Arabic-speaking nomadic tribes, with weapons and equipment for coordinated attacks on the ground. The resulting campaign of ethnic cleansing has killed more than 200,000 civilians and displaced more than 1.6 million people. Some 200,000 additional refugees have fled across the border into Chad to escape the violence.

Given the scope of the conflict, the prosecutor's investigation has been wide-ranging. He inherited the evidence collected by the UN International Commission and developed additional information from new witnesses and experts. Owing to security concerns and the Sudanese government's opposition to the investigation, the Court's investigators have operated almost entirely outside of Darfur. Nonetheless, in February 2007 the prosecutor applied for warrants against two individuals alleged to be among the most responsible for the crimes committed in Darfur: Ahmad Muhammad Harun, a former government minister for internal affairs; and Ali Kushayb, a Janjaweed leader aligned with the government. The warrants were issued three months later and listed fifty-one counts of war crimes and crimes against humanity, including persecution, murder and attacks against civilians, forcible transfer, rape, pillaging, destruction of property, inhumane acts, imprisonment, and torture.

The Sudanese government announced that it would not deliver Harun, Kushayb, or any other Sudanese national to the Court, arguing that the charges were politically motivated. But the prosecutor went further. In July 2008 he announced his intention to indict the president of Sudan, Omar al-Bashir, on charges of genocide, crimes against humanity, and war crimes. The Court rejected the count of genocide but confirmed the other charges in February 2009. The warrant constitutes the ICC's first indictment of a sitting head of state.

The prosecutor also sought charges against rebel commanders in Darfur. In November 2008 he announced that he had applied for warrants against three unnamed rebel leaders for their role in a September 2007 attack that killed twelve African Union peacekeepers. The warrant application listed three counts of war crimes, including murder and causing severe injury to peacekeepers, intentionally directing attacks against personnel and property involved in a peacekeeping mission, and pillaging.

Central African Republic

In May 2007, the prosecutor began an investigation in the Central African Republic, more than two years after the government of the Central African Republic referred for investigation "crimes within the jurisdiction of the Court committed anywhere on [its] territory . . . since 1 July 2002." Violence in the CAR began in 2001, when President Ange-Félix Patassé invited the Mouvement de Libération du Congo (MLC), an armed group operating in the DRC, to assist him in efforts to defeat a coup attempt. The move led to fierce fighting but ultimately was unsuccessful: Patassé's government fell in March 2003, and former Armed Forces chief of staff François Bozizé came to power. When the prosecutor launched his investigation into crimes in the CAR, he noted that it likely would focus on sexual violence during this period, "as allegations of sexual crimes far outnumber alleged killings."

The investigation in the CAR has resulted in one arrest so far. In May 2008 the prosecutor sought, and the Court issued, an arrest warrant for Jean-Pierre Bemba Gombo, a current senator and former vice president of the DRC and chairman of the MLC, the armed group that operated in the CAR from 2001 to 2003. The warrant charged Bemba with two counts of crimes against humanity and four counts of war crimes, including rape, torture, outrages upon personal dignity, and pillaging. The charges relate to the commission of hundreds of rapes and gender-based crimes against the civilian population of Bangui. According to the prosecutor, Bemba "pursued a plan of terrorizing and brutalizing innocent civilians, in particular during a campaign of massive rapes and looting."

Bemba was arrested in Belgium shortly after the warrant was issued. After what the prosecutor called "a complex and well-prepared operation," the Belgian government transferred him to the Court. Bemba's arrest was notable as the first time a state had detained a foreigner solely on the basis of a warrant from the Court. Also notable was the action of the Portuguese government, taken two months after Bemba's arrest, to seize his property. This measure reportedly came at the request of the Court, and the confiscated property included his mansion, yacht, private plane, and two luxury cars.

INTERNATIONAL REACTION TO THE COURT'S ACTIONS

The processes by which these cases have come before the Court themselves provide an indication of international support for the work of the Court. State Parties and the UN Security Council encouraged the prosecutor to open the current investigations, and he has pursued them with their continued support. The governments of Uganda, DRC, and CAR each requested the Court's assistance, specifically referring crimes in their own territory for investigation. While each had its own reasons for turning to the Court, these self-referrals signaled the countries' concern about domestic capacity for and credibility of prosecution, recognition of the gravity of the crimes that had occurred, and confidence in the ICC. Although these countries were members of the Court when they referred their situations to the prosecutor, they were under no obligation to do so. Conversely, support for the Darfur investigation came not from Sudan but from the UN Security Council. The unopposed Security Council resolution was a signal of support for the work of the Court and a potential precedent.

Many states have taken concrete steps to support the Court's investigations: the United Nations and the European Union signed cooperation agreements with the Court; several states negotiated similar agreements or ad hoc arrangements with the prosecutor; and, according to the prosecutor, a number of nations have "provided timely information." So far, two State Parties—Belgium and the DRC—have arrested and transferred suspects to the Court, and the prosecutor has said that Portugal "worked for months to prepare [Bemba's] arrest." Portugal, the DRC, and Belgium also facilitated execution of the Court's search warrants. France provided transport for Lubanga to the Court, and the United Nations has supported the Court by providing information and documentation in his case.

The Darfur case is the most indicative of the growing importance of the Court. Rather than create an ad hoc tribunal as the UN Security Council had done in the 1990s in the case of former Yugoslavia and Rwanda, the council voted to confer jurisdiction on the ICC. The prosecutor's investigation palpably changed the dynamics of the Darfur crisis. The Court's announcement of arrest warrants for a Sudanese government official and militia leader focused additional attention on the conflict and led to an intense period of diplomacy. Sudan's allies came to its defense. Critics of the Khartoum government applauded the move toward accountability. The diplomatic flurry intensified after the prosecutor targeted Bashir himself.

The Court has helped to hasten progress toward ending atrocities and encouraged accountability for grave crimes in indirect ways as well. In Uganda, for example, the announcement of the prosecutor's investigation helped bring the LRA back to the negotiating table for the most serious peace talks ever pursued in the twenty-year conflict, splintered the leadership, and arguably contributed to the decisions of mid-level officers to lay down their weapons and accept the outstanding offer of amnesty from the government. As noted, concerns over disloyalty led Kony to order the execution of the group's second-in-command, the LRA's most experienced military strategist. Negotiations between the LRA and the Ugandan government ended when Kony repeatedly failed to sign a peace agreement negotiated by intermediaries he had appointed. Still, the war has effectively ended in northern Uganda, where displaced populations are now returning home. Full exploration of a negotiated peace also enabled the countries in the region, where civilian populations remain threatened by the LRA—Uganda, the Sudan, and the Congo—to reach a new consensus that the LRA, now operating mainly in the Congo, should be routed through joint military efforts. If Kony or the other LRA leaders named in the ICC warrants should be apprehended, they could be prosecuted before the ICC, or in Uganda, where the ICC's intervention prompted proposals for a domestic mechanism to investigate and prosecute atrocities.

Signs of progress also are apparent in the DRC. For example, Human Rights Watch has reported that soon after the Court announced its investigation in June 2005, government and rebel military leaders warned their troops not to direct attacks at civilians or commit war crimes out of fear of prosecution. In 2006, after Lubanga was transferred to The Hague, militia leaders throughout the country expressed fears of arrest and reported that they did not want to "end up like Lubanga." In response, some of these commanders claimed a desire to launch investigations into crimes committed by their troops, perhaps hoping to avoid prosecution for their troops' crimes under doctrines of command responsibility. Human Rights Watch also found that the Lubanga case raised awareness more generally among the Congolese people about the consequences of recruiting and enlisting children into the military and reduced the likelihood that families would volunteer their children to serve in a militia.

Positive developments have not been limited to countries where the Court is conducting active investigations. Kenya, for example, experienced widespread violence following its national elections in December 2007. Although more than 1,000 civilians died and more than 300,000 were displaced from their homes, the toll could have been worse; reports suggest that potential prosecution by the Court deterred some ethnic leaders from inciting further hostilities. More concretely, after the violence ended, the Court became a catalyst for domestic efforts at accountability. A neutral commission appointed to investigate the postelection violence recommended that a special domestic tribunal be established to prosecute crimes against humanity or that the matter be forwarded to the ICC. The recommendation had teeth: the commission gathered the names of approximately ten individuals it believed were most responsible for atrocities; the names were not released publicly but sealed in an envelope left with former UN secretary general Kofi Annan for safekeeping. The commission threatened to forward the names to the ICC prosecutor if a domestic tribunal was not established within sixty days. Facing this ultimatum, the coalition government agreed in December 2008 to establish a Special Tribunal that will apply both Kenyan and international criminal law to prosecute the worst perpetrators of violence in the postelection period.

Protection of Defendants' Rights

With the engagement of the Pre-Trial, Trial, and Appeals Chambers, the Court's judges have construed the Rome Statute and rules broadly to protect the rights of defendants. They have done this in part by ensuring that the defense perspective is heard on contested matters even before a defendant has been named. For example, when the prosecutor sought forensic examinations in the DRC pursuant to Article 56, which governs the collection of evidence during a "unique investigative opportunity," the Pre-Trial Chamber appointed an ad hoc counsel to represent defense interests. The judges in the Uganda and Darfur cases have taken a similar approach on victims' issues, appointing defense counsel to litigate matters related to the role of victims in the proceedings.

The Court's judges have taken serious steps, often controversial, to protect defendants. The most public example was the suspension of the case against Lubanga over concerns that the prosecutor was withholding exculpatory evidence from the defense. The dispute concerned Articles 54(3)(e) and 67(2) of the Rome Statute: the first provision allows the prosecutor to agree not to disclose confidential information he receives only for the purpose of generating leads unless the information-provider consents to disclosure. The second demands that the prosecutor disclose evidence tending to "mitigate the guilt of the accused." The Court was called upon to rule on the means of harmonizing these provisions in the Lubanga case, as some of the material the prosecutor received on the condition of confidentiality contained information also conceded by the prosecutor to be potentially exonerating. When the prosecutor advanced the argument that the material at issue could not be disclosed for judicial review, the judges ordered a halt to the trial. After a lengthy delay, the prosecutor's sources agreed to allow disclosure to the Trial Chamber, and defense counsel were permitted to examine the potentially exculpatory evidence. In the meantime, the judges' decision to delay the trial signaled clearly their willingness to end a case if necessary to safeguard a defendant's right to a fair trial.

Promotion of "Complementarity" Principles and Victims' Voice

The Court's judges have repeatedly emphasized that the complementarity principle of Article 17(1)(a) permits national investigations and prosecutions to preempt and preclude action by the Court. For national proceedings to do so, they must include "both the person and the conduct which is the subject of the case before the Court." If the requirements of Article 17(1)(a) are met, the Court has acknowledged that it would have no authority to proceed with a trial.

Because of these limits, the judges have paid close attention to developments in countries where the Court is active. The judges considering the Uganda case sought clarification from the Ugandan government after news reports indicated that it intended to establish a domestic tribunal for members of the LRA as part of a comprehensive peace agreement then under consideration. The judges also initiated status conferences to keep abreast of the negotiations with the LRA, implying that they would consider domestic justice efforts when determining whether any future trials could proceed against indicted LRA leaders. To date, the judges have determined that the Ugandan initiatives do not preclude prosecution of the indicted LRA leaders, although defense attorneys have appealed the decision and the judges could revisit it in the future. In Sudan, the government has announced that it is investigating the alleged crimes there and opposes the Court's involvement. The judges have held status conferences on the issue and expect to consider under the provisions of Article 17 whether Sudan's efforts are genuine or intended instead to shield perpetrators from prosecution by the ICC.

When the Rome Statute was drafted, many praised the inclusion of provisions to protect victims of atrocities. For example, Articles 57(3)(c) and 64(6)(e) empower the Pre-Trial and Trial Chambers respectively to "provide for the protection . . . of victims," and Article 68 states that, "where the personal interests of the victims are affected, the Court shall permit their views and concerns to be presented and considered." The DRC and Uganda cases immediately presented the Court with the question of how to apply these principles in practice. With assistance from Court-appointed counsel, victims have applied for the right to participate in proceedings, and have been represented and expressed views through their legal representatives at pre-trial proceedings, during the Lubanga trial, and in certain interlocutory appeals. Victims now routinely submit filings on contested trial and pre-trial issues that affect their interests.

The Court's judges have been careful to enforce protection obligations for victims. A great deal of time and attention has been given to implementing protection measures, such as redaction, anonymity, or other methods to shield identity (including at trial) and witness relocation and protection.

Operational Issues

As a practical matter, the Court has been able to make progress because its operational foundation is firmly in place. In a few short years, the Court's staff has grown from zero to include nearly 700 permanent positions spread across its four organs: the presidency, which includes the judges who are the president and first and second vice presidents; the Chambers, which include the judges; the Office of the Prosecutor, which includes lawyers and investigators; and the Registry, which handles the administrative workload of the Court in addition to specific roles in areas as diverse as public relations and witness security. The Court's budget now exceeds 100 million euros, and progress is being made on securing permanent premises in The Hague. The Court also has established six field offices, including a liaison office in New York to handle business at the United Nations. Even the mundane demonstrates the scope of the Court's activity: officials already have produced almost 25,000 pages of court documents and held more than fifty-five judicial sessions.

These details demonstrate that the Court is more than a fragile treaty organization; it increasingly acts as an international institution. Its reach cannot be attributed to increasing budgets and bricks and mortar. Its influence has grown as well. The mention of a potential investigation by the prosecutor sends diplomats scrambling. Some of this attention flows from the nature of the cases themselves; some can be attributed to the Security Council referral in the Darfur case. But a substantial amount of the focus on the Court derives from its unique role as a permanent court focused on the important task of investigating and prosecuting gross violations of human rights beyond the boundaries of national criminal justice systems. Many nongovernmental organizations address human rights issues and campaign for victims of atrocities. But their role is different; they are advocates, and thanks to them human rights is now an integral part of the international discussion. They are, however, in no position, and of course lack the authority, to adjudicate criminal conduct. For that a court is required.

CRITICISMS OF THE COURT'S OPERATION

Critics charge that the Court is unduly focused on Africa. All of the investigations launched by the prosecutor concern situations on that continent: Uganda, the DRC, Sudan, and the CAR. Critics find the limited scope of the Court's caseload troubling. Some claim that the Court, based in Europe, is attempting to reassert a form of colonial supervision over the continent; others argue that the prosecutions reinforce a negative stereotype of Africa as a collection of failed states and civil wars. In short, the Court's focus on Africa, critics say, reflects an intentional strategy rather than chance.

Of course, it is not chance. But neither does it seem to be at all nefarious. Three of the four countries where the prosecutor has launched investigations invited his efforts; the fourth was the product of a UN Security Council resolution. And the Court's temporal jurisdiction, which prevents it from prosecuting crimes that occurred before July 2002, places a practical constraint on opportunities for investigation by the Court. During the seven-year period when the Court has had jurisdiction, grave crimes have occurred worldwide, but Africa has seen a disproportionate share of the violence. More than any other factor, the Court's caseload reflects this imbalance, as well as the absence of judicial capacity in some parts of the continent.

A broader criticism along the same lines is that the Court is not immune to considerations of realpolitik. The goal of putting an end to impunity, though neutral and universal in the abstract, has been more selective in the pursuit, with situations in weaker or smaller states more likely to attract the Court's attention than situations involving great powers. There is potential truth to this claim, but those who advance it should be explicit about what they seek. Do they want a free pass for all perpetrators of atrocities until every such perpetrator can be held to account? Is there a plausible way to a world in which all perpetrators are held to account except by way of a world in which *increasing numbers* of perpetrators are held to account?

The prosecutor's investigations in Uganda and Sudan also have stirred controversy as to whether they are obstacles to peace. Some observers fear that the Court's investigations in these countries are doing more harm than good. Both countries are engaged in armed conflicts within their borders, Sudan with rebel groups in its Darfur region and Uganda with the LRA in the northern part of the country.[2] The toll on innocent civilians in both countries is high, and both governments have engaged in efforts to negotiate an end to the conflicts. Although these negotiations no doubt would be difficult in any circumstance, the Court's arrest warrants complicate matters considerably. In Uganda, the leadership of the LRA faces prosecution; in Sudan, a government official and an allied militia leader, as well as the president himself, are vulnerable to arrest. The LRA responded to the warrants by demanding that any peace deal include a promise of immunity from the Court. Without such protection, the group said, it would continue to fight. Sudan's Bashir has also made explicit threats and ordered the departure of aid organizations from Darfur immediately after the warrant for his arrest was issued by the Court. He has also thumbed his nose at the legitimacy of the Court by attending the summit of the Arab League in Doha in March while under indictment. The Bashir government has called the Court illegitimate, and some regional leaders have expressed fear that a durable peace in Darfur is not possible with the shadow of prosecution looming over the government. In addition, there is concern that the indictment of Bashir imperils the hard-won but fragile North-South peace agreement, which ended a twenty-year civil war that claimed over 2 million lives. The resulting dilemma is often phrased as one of peace versus justice, with critics concerned that the pursuit of justice in countries like Sudan and Uganda impedes the path to peace. We will return to this subject in the next chapter. For now, we readily acknowledge that this is a very serious question and one to which only a partial response is possible so far.

Finally, the Court's arrest record has been disappointing, although this cannot be blamed on the Court, which has no police force and must rely on the cooperation of states and others to carry out the arrests. Only four of the twelve individuals indicted by the Court have been arrested and transferred to its custody, and two of those four already were in custody in the Congo on other charges when the Court issued its arrest warrants. And there is little reason to be optimistic about future arrests. Warrants for the five LRA leaders in Uganda have been outstanding since 2005 without any discernible sign of progress, although two of the five are believed dead. The Sudanese government has declared that it will not cooperate with any request for arrest. As a result, unless support for arrest efforts increases among states and international organizations, future arrests are most likely to occur in a manner similar to that of Bemba, who was arrested abroad when he traveled to a second home. For now, such arrests seem more likely than catching the Court's fugitives on their own turf.

Taken as a whole, the Court has faced many challenges, but the difficulties it confronts tend to be different from the concerns lodged in the United States by the Court's critics. With respect to the U.S. concerns, the Court's record belies many of the objections raised by its critics. The prosecutor has rejected frivolous referrals. Since July 2002, he has received more than 2,200 reports of alleged crimes under the Court's jurisdiction. Although these communications have come from more than 100 different countries, individuals and groups from the United States, the United Kingdom, France, and Germany are responsible for 60 percent of them. These reports alleged crimes in 139 countries, spanning all the regions of the world. The prosecutor found 80 percent to be manifestly outside the Court's jurisdiction and not worthy of additional analysis, while 20 percent merited a closer look. Fewer than a dozen of those have been subject to intensive analysis, and of those only four have resulted in investigation. A number of situations remain under investigation, including alleged crimes committed in Afghanistan, Colombia, Kenya, Georgia, and Chad. The prosecutor has also said that he will "respond" to a communication from the Palestinian Authority about Israeli conduct in Gaza in 2009.

Notably, the prosecutor has yet to bring a case on his own initiative, which he has the power to do under Article 15. On the contrary, he has declined investigations in two cases that could have proven controversial: Iraq and Venezuela. In Venezuela, the prosecutor stated that the alleged crimes against humanity were not widespread or systematic, and the elements of the crimes were not met.

The request for an Iraq investigation was obviously of special interest to the United States. The prosecutor rebuffed an opportunity to open an official investigation into crimes by coalition forces in Iraq. After receiving more than 200 communications alleging war crimes, crimes against humanity, and genocide, the prosecutor responded with a detailed ten-page letter citing three primary reasons for not moving forward. First, the prosecutor noted that, because Iraq is not a signatory to the Rome Statute and has not consented to the Court's jurisdiction, he could investigate and prosecute only individuals who are nationals of a State Party. For practical purposes, this decision limited the prosecutor's review of alleged crimes to those committed by British troops, who are subject to the Court's jurisdiction because the United Kingdom has signed the Rome Statute, removing American activities from even preliminary scrutiny. Second, the prosecutor concluded that, based on the facts available and public reports, there was insufficient evidence, or "no reasonable indicia," that crimes against humanity or genocide had occurred. Finally, although there was a reasonable basis to conclude that some war crimes had been committed—including the willful killing of civilians—the prosecutor determined that the number of victims and scope of alleged crimes fell below the threshold necessary to prompt the Court's involvement. In making this determination, he noted that his estimate of the "number of potential victims of crimes within the jurisdiction of the Court . . . was of a different order than the number of victims found in other situations under investigation or analysis by the Office," such as the thousands of willful killings and millions of civilians displaced in Uganda, the DRC, and Darfur. The prosecutor also noted that national proceedings were under way regarding potential crimes involving prisoner mistreatment. The prosecutor's letter clarified his position on a number of issues that have been debated in the United States. For example, the prosecutor explained that "the International Criminal Court has a mandate to examine the *conduct during the conflict*, but not whether the *decision to engage* in armed conflict was legal."[3]

As a result, he could not and did not conduct any inquiry into how the Iraq war began. He also made clear that, "under international humanitarian law and the Rome Statute, the death of civilians during an armed conflict, no matter how grave and regrettable, does not in itself constitute a war crime." The prosecutor's treatment of this issue demonstrated that he would consider seriously the protections employed by the military to reduce civilian deaths. In his letter, the prosecutor noted favorably a number of measures undertaken by the British Army, including the provision of legal advice to military leaders, the "political, legal and military oversight . . . established for target approval," and the use of detailed computer modeling and real-time information to assess targets. In addition, the prosecutor indicated that he would and did provide national governments with an opportunity to respond to allegations. The United Kingdom forwarded such a response, which he took into consideration and referenced in his letter. The prosecutor's actions in this matter belied many of the concerns critics have expressed about how the office would handle oversight of military action.

Similarly, the Court has not exercised jurisdiction over non-party nationals except at the request of the UN Security Council. As detailed above, all the defendants already before the Court are nationals of State Parties with the exception of the Sudanese defendants. There, the Security Council granted the Court jurisdiction over crimes in Darfur in much the same manner that it had done for crimes in the former Yugoslavia and Rwanda, albeit to a permanent criminal tribunal rather than a temporary one. Moreover, the governments of Uganda, the DRC, and CAR not only ratified the Rome Statute, they also requested explicitly that the Prosecutor and the Court be involved in their affairs.

Finally, contrary to critics' worst fears, the prosecutor has maintained a friendly relationship with the United States. During his term in office he has regularly visited the United States. Since taking office in 2003, Ocampo has given informal briefings to members of Congress, taught classes at Harvard Law School, and appeared at numerous conferences in New York, Chicago, and Washington. Less apparent but equally revealing has been his recruitment of American lawyers for key staff positions. For example, Ocampo made news when he hired a former federal prosecutor from New York to serve as the senior trial attorney supervising the Court's first investigation. Since that attorney's departure the prosecutor has continuously had at least one former American prosecutor on his senior staff. Such moves are far removed from the caricature of an anti-American prosecutor using the Court to pursue a political agenda.

PEACE VERSUS PROSECUTION

The prosecutor's investigations in Uganda and Sudan also have stirred controversy as to whether they impede the path to peace. Both countries are engaged in armed conflicts within their borders, Sudan with rebel groups in its Darfur region and Uganda with the LRA in the northern part of the country. Although any peace negotiations would be difficult in these circumstances, some observers fear that the Court's investigations are doing more harm than good. In their view, the Court's pursuit of justice should wait for stability or be used as barter in the context of peace negotiations. They contend that warrants will only extend the conflicts, provoke violent responses from the targets, and cause innocent civilians to suffer even more. Others critics point to more political problems, such as the lack of alternatives available to diplomats to resolve conflicts after the Court intervenes, and problems created by a perception of outside meddling in regional affairs.

The resulting dilemma is often framed as one of peace versus justice or peace versus prosecution. Without question, there are competing goods in play in these situations. We reject an approach that seeks a categorical "solution" to the problem, however, as if it were a matter of simply choosing peace or accountability. In the real world, these values are often as interrelated as they are in conflict, and the policy choices must and will reflect the specific circumstances of the case in question. You do not necessarily secure peace by forgoing the concern for justice; nor do indictments and warrants necessarily impede (or advance) the cause of peace. Neither of the extreme positions—that we must forgo peace in the interest of accountability, or that we must forgo accountability in the interest of peace—is of much practical use as a general guide for policymakers.

To be sure, the Court's involvement in ongoing conflicts can complicate matters. In Uganda, for example, the entire top leadership of the LRA faces prosecution. In Sudan, the indicted president is now vulnerable to arrest. The LRA responded to the Court's warrants by demanding that any peace deal include a promise of immunity from the Court. Without such protection, the group said it would continue to fight. Sudan temporarily expelled foreign aid groups and has already ousted many, prosecuted alleged ICC "informers," and increased its rhetoric against the Court. Many regional leaders fear that a durable peace in Darfur is not possible with the warrant looming over Bashir.

The Court's actions can and will have real, often human, costs. The likes of Kony and Bashir will continue to take innocent lives until someone stops them. But many of the critics display an unyielding attention to the short-term effects of the Court's investigations—what will happen tomorrow, next week, and next month. It is easy to understand this perspective, because many critics are on the front lines of conflicts and observe their horrors on a daily basis. Yet the situation in Darfur was hardly on a path toward resolution either before the referral to the ICC or before the Court issued the warrant for Bashir. The current regime in Khartoum came to power via a bloody coup, conducted a brutal civil war against its southern population in part by bombing civilians, used famine as a weapon by restricting aid agencies' access to famine-stricken areas, and permitted slavery to flourish across parts of the country. Yet in each case President Bashir and his government managed to do just enough to keep the international community at bay. The lesson he and his regime have learned over the years is simple: violate human rights first, tell the international community you're sorry later. Unless and until this cycle is broken, leaders like Bashir will have no incentive *not* to engage in practices—like forced displacement of civilians or rape as a weapon of war—that have proved so successful at helping them maintain power. The consequences are equally grave in Uganda. As one commentator put it, "If Kony's attempt to gain immunity succeeds . . . warlords will gain confidence that, if armed rebellion fails, they can leverage brutality to dictate the terms of their surrender."[4]

In addition, international diplomacy has been shaped by the issuance of the warrant for Bashir. While the African Union and the Arab League have rallied around Bashir, the European Union has hardened its position and is now demanding that Bashir accept a comprehensive settlement before it will consider an Article 16 deferral. At this writing in 2009, the U.S. and EU positions are now more closely aligned on the Darfur issue than at any previous time. The transatlantic alignment has shaped the Security Council dynamic, with the potential to erode Russian and especially Chinese opposition to strong action.

The brief history of the Court suggests that the threat of prosecution has affected the calculations of rank-and-file troops and their leaders. For example, Human Rights Watch has reported that, soon after the Court announced its investigation in June 2005, government and rebel military leaders in Sudan warned their troops not to direct attacks at civilians or commit war crimes out of fear of prosecution.[5] As noted, some DRC militia leaders worried about sharing Lubanga's fate. These effects have not been limited to countries where the Court is conducting active investigations. Kenya, for example, experienced widespread violence following its national elections in December 2007. Although more than 1,000 civilians died and more than 300,000 were displaced from their homes, the toll could have been worse, and some accounts indicate that potential prosecution by the Court dissuaded some ethnic leaders from inciting further hostilities.

Moreover, the Court's involvement in situations of ongoing atrocities can change the dynamic on the ground for the better. The Uganda case is a prime example. The announcement of the prosecutor's investigation brought the LRA back to the negotiating table and directly contributed to the decisions of dozens of mid-level officers to lay down their weapons and accept an outstanding amnesty offer by the government. Facing indictment, the group's leadership splintered. As noted, concerns over disloyalty led to the execution of the group's second-in-command. Another commander reportedly began to consider abandoning the rebel group. Although negotiations between the LRA and the Ugandan government have yet to result in a stable peace agreement, the process has resulted in less violence and more stability in the affected parts of the country.

The Court's presence also has encouraged domestic efforts at accountability. This has been particularly true in Uganda, where debate over the Court's warrants has focused attention on the need for accountability and led to proposals for a domestic mechanism to investigate and prosecute atrocities. In Kenya, the Court became a counterweight for proponents of a domestic justice mechanism. A neutral commission appointed to investigate the postelection violence in the country recommended that a special domestic tribunal be established to prosecute crimes against humanity or that the matter be forwarded to the ICC. These were not idle words. In a bold move, the commission, as noted above, confidentially gathered the names of those believed most responsible for atrocities and threatened to turn the list over to the ICC unless the Kenyan government acted, which it did.

While the prosecutor's role is clearly to pursue accountability within his authority under the Rome Statute, it is naive to suppose that the occupant of such a position will be oblivious to the international environment in which he is operating. It is not the job of the prosecutor to wheel and deal in pursuit of progress toward peace and reconciliation, of course. But an acute sense of the nuances of diplomacy ought to be a requirement for the position, and the ICC ought to see itself and be seen in the context of broader international efforts to end conflicts and save lives.

CHAPTER FIVE

THE AMERICAN INTEREST IN INTERNATIONAL JUSTICE

THERE ARE NUMEROUS potential perspectives from which to view the International Criminal Court. Some of its most ardent advocates, for example, see the Court as an essential element in the architecture of global governance. If the United Nations (at least in aspiration) serves as "the parliament of man" (the phrase of Lord Tennyson that the scholar Paul Kennedy selected for the title of his book celebrating the promise of the United Nations), then the ICC is the supreme court of accountability for violation of international criminal law.

Others would go still further: in the long run, the United Nations Security Council itself is a dubious institution because of the special privileges of the five permanent members. The veto power is, in this view, an instrument for the protection of self-interest over and above considerations of justice. Hence the unwillingness of many nongovernmental organizations and "like-minded states" at the time of the final drafting of the Rome

Statute to *require* the Court's cases to be referred by the Security Council. The Court's prosecutor, in this view, needed the authority to act on his own motion (with the approval of a Court review panel of judges) precisely because there might be instances in which one or more of the veto powers would block action, thereby trumping accountability and returning to a doctrine of impunity for the privileged.

This ambitious view of the Court has in turn provoked a counterattack. Some see the Court as an instrument designed to hobble the freedom of action of the United States. They see the Court as a threat, at least in principle and certainly by the avowed aspiration of some proponents, to the sovereignty of the United States and other sovereign states—indeed, to the modern Westphalian state system. In this view, the United States should stay as far away as possible from the ICC. Whether or not the Court has the intention of hauling senior U.S. officials or military commanders into its chambers on trumped-up charges of war crimes, the Court is a trap, in this view—a step on a slippery slope toward "global government" or rulemaking on an international scale by unelected and unaccountable judges and bureaucrats.

These perspectives and the conclusions that follow from them deserve respect, whether one agrees with them or not. They are not, however, the perspective from which we have tried to examine the question of the International Criminal Court in this book. The question here is whether a new policy of cooperation with the Court serves U.S. interests. It is a practical question born of a pragmatic approach to policymaking. It is not merely a theoretical or hypothetical question, as the Court through its operation has made a record that needs to be examined open-mindedly.

Although ideological perspectives serve the end of clarifying basic principles and of illuminating the ways in which principles sometimes come into conflict, it is important to bear in mind that the orientation of the policymaker is largely consequentialist. That does not make policymakers unprincipled (at least not necessarily). But they tend to think about what they should do by asking whether the likely consequences of policy X will be, on net, good or bad for the country. Such a process requires good information, sound analysis, historical perspective, experience, and good judgment. In most cases, the more thoroughly that alternative points of view and "what if" scenarios are explored and assumptions questioned, the better the chance of a good outcome. Reasonable people will still end up reaching different conclusions, and not infrequently. We hope this book makes a contribution to officials making policy on international justice and the Court.

We see the International Criminal Court as, potentially, a means to an end. The end is not "global governance," a perspective we reject as the lens through which to evaluate the utility and efficacy of the Court. The end is holding perpetrators of atrocities to account for their actions. Our conclusion is that a new policy of cooperation with the International Criminal Court will serve that end better than the alternatives of (1) a policy of hostility to the Court, in which the United States actively seeks to undermine its operations; (2) a policy of "benign neglect" of the Court, according to which the United States largely ignores the Court, does not seek to bring clarity to the U.S. position, and deals with the Court as necessary on an ad hoc basis; or (3) a policy of swiftly seeking approval of the Rome Statute by the U.S. Senate so that the United States becomes a State Party and a member of the Court's governing Assembly. In this chapter, we explain why this policy of cooperation makes the most sense among the available options—why, that is, the United States has *an interest* in cooperating with the International Criminal Court.

The United States has long had and continues to have a strong moral strain in its foreign policy. This strain holds, among other things, that perpetrators of mass atrocities need to be held to account and punished. Although the United States remains zealous in defense of its sovereign rights as a general principle, the U.S. government has rejected the proposition that one can use sovereignty as a shield to create impunity for atrocities. The United States, by declaration and action, has supported accountability across national boundaries in a variety of forms.

A court alone cannot stop atrocities, and the ICC has confronted and will continue to confront the political realities that will prevent it from pursuing atrocities in every country in which they occur. It is true that the ICC has not set its sights on situations involving great powers. The objection that the ICC acts only against weak and convenient targets needs to be taken seriously. However, the inability of the ICC to prosecute all crimes is not an argument against the prosecution of any crimes. It has been no small advance for victims in those weak and convenient targets to at last have a court with the potential to prosecute *génocidaires*. To the extent that the Court also deters would-be perpetrators, that is valuable even if perpetrators are not universally deterred. Those who seek to hold perpetrators to account must also attend to the hard political work of preventing or stopping the atrocities and apprehending those responsible. This can be difficult and dangerous, and success is not guaranteed. Yet the United States has never been and should not be satisfied with anything like the conclusion that once a matter has been referred to an international court it has thereby been resolved. At the same time, it is now almost inconceivable that the United States, acting with others or on its own to stop unfolding atrocity crimes, would then fail to put in place some juridical procedure for holding to account violators of the laws of war or international humanitarian law.

As we have seen, the United States has supported the creation of special tribunals when circumstances demanded. When faced with a similar situation of mass atrocities in the Darfur region of Sudan, and with the International Criminal Court having become operational, the United States abstained and thus allowed to pass a Security Council referral of the situation there to the ICC. It seems likely that the need for some sort of international tribunal to adjudicate an atrocity case will arise again. Provided the ICC is no less effective in pursuit of its mandate than the ad hoc tribunals have been, it would seem to be wasteful of resources to create a new ad hoc tribunal rather than to turn once again to the ICC.

It might have made sense for the United States to abstain on the Darfur referral rather than vote in favor of it, given the unprecedented nature of the action and the state of ICC policy in the Bush administration. But if circumstances arise again for a Security Council referral, the Darfur referral will be the precedent, and U.S. policy will have been modified at least to the extent of having allowed the Darfur referral to go through. If, in the view of U.S. policymakers, the prosecutor through his own fault had somehow bungled the Darfur case in a fashion that discredited the Court in U.S. eyes, then it might be reasonable to return to ad hoc tribunals. But the Bush administration itself repeatedly expressed support for the prosecutor in the Darfur case, and the Obama administration did so at the Security Council in the maiden speech of the new U.S. permanent representative to the United Nations. The ICC is now the logical default option when an international tribunal is necessary, even for the United States as a non-party to the Rome Statute. The ICC will remain so for as long as it remains effective within the limits of possibility. (It would be an error of judgment to blame the ICC when the pursuit of justice as such in a particular case turns out to be difficult, such as with the apprehension of indicted fugitives by police or military personnel of governments.)

If the non-party United States, too, has come to rely on the ICC and to express support for the prosecutor's work, it is hard to imagine why the U.S. government wouldn't do everything it reasonably can to support the investigations the prosecutor is undertaking. The United States wants not just *de minimis* investigations but investigations that are as rigorous and complete as possible. The United States is in a position to be helpful to the prosecutor across a range of activities, as we discuss in chapter 6. It only makes sense to provide assistance, and to remove any existing impediments in U.S. law to that end.

Insofar as the United States seeks to deter would-be perpetrators of mass atrocities, a functioning international court combined with international will to halt atrocities and detain perpetrators may play a role. Certainly most Americans would agree that fear of punishment deters crime in the United States and other countries. It is doubtful that the certainty or swiftness of international justice will ever have as strong a deterrent effect as do those qualities in domestic criminal justice systems in strong states, but anecdotal evidence suggests that a deterrent effect in some local circumstances is already noticeable. It is reasonable to suppose that the stronger and more manifest the international commitment to hold perpetrators to account, the greater the deterrent effect will be.

If the United States has an interest in upholding an important moral dimension of its foreign policy by seeking to hold perpetrators of mass atrocities to account across international borders if need be, and if the ICC has a certain practical claim to be the most logical vehicle for the pursuit of this interest, we still have to consider fully whether there might be flaws in the ICC so grave that the costs of U.S. cooperation with the Court would outweigh the benefits to the United States of cooperation.

The ICC is here to stay. The Court is a permanent fixture of the international system to the extent that the system can be said to have any such fixtures. The United Nations came into being following the devastation of the Second World War. It would probably take upheaval on a similar scale to lead to its abandonment for the creation of a new body along the same or different lines, or to a decision that the world is better off without such a body. The same is likely true of the International Criminal Court. International conflict on a scale that might lead to the dismantling of the current Court is something we expect even the Court's staunchest opponents would agree is undesirable.

The ICC was a long time in the creation, and though the treaty terms establishing it were, in the U.S. view, seriously flawed, there is no realistic prospect of starting all over. The states that overwhelmingly adopted the treaty in Rome over U.S. objections were largely satisfied with their handiwork, and support for the Court among them has not diminished since then; on the contrary, it appears to have grown. With Chile's ratification in June 2009, there are now a total of 109 states that are party to the treaty. Obviously, the parties recognize that there is room for improvement in the operation of the Court, a prospect the Rome Statute itself holds open. But there is no sentiment for returning to the negotiating table to reopen the treaty and address basic U.S. concerns. The Court is fully operational in accordance with the terms of the Rome Statute, and the United States should accept this international fact of life. The United States cannot reasonably expect to undo the ICC.

The ICC, in its operations so far, has embraced the role of "court of last resort." It has been deferential to national courts, as the Rome Statute requires, even in the case of Sudan. Neither the prosecutor nor the judges on the Court have tried to supersede local juridical arrangements for holding perpetrators of crimes to account. Although some may have hoped the Court would take on an activist role, perhaps through the authority of the prosecutor to begin investigations on his own motion, the Court has not taken shape as a politicized body outside its juridical function. It has not become subservient to extra-juridical agendas.

U.S. officials and military commanders and troops are at little and diminishing risk of being held to account at the ICC. In the first place, the U.S. military works diligently to conduct the horrendous business of waging war in a way that minimizes risks to civilians. Incidents have occurred and will no doubt never completely vanish, but the institutional culture of the military is geared to civilian protection, not abuse, and the legal code governing conduct at war provides for severe punishment for perpetrators of atrocities. Civilian prosecutors acting in the name of the people are also capable of investigating allegations of civilian war crimes should the need arise, and U.S. courts have ample capacity to try such cases. The gaps remaining between international legal codification of crimes subject to prosecution and U.S. law making such activities criminal offenses have been identified by U.S. lawmakers, who are working in bipartisan fashion to close them. The Court has already declined to investigate allegations that soldiers who were nationals of State Parties (including the British) perpetrated or aided the perpetration of war crimes in Iraq in part on grounds that the domestic system at issue had the capacity to address any such crimes in their own systems.

The adoption of the Rome Statute in 1998, including the seven years (at the time of this writing) in which the Court has been operational following the required number of ratifications by signatories, constitutes a historical record that must count for something. By all accounts, the Court has been scrupulous in the development of its internal policies and procedures, and although the results are, unsurprisingly, not entirely the same as the procedural rules of U.S. courts, they certainly meet or exceed any reasonable international standard for legitimacy. The prosecutor, similarly, has been scrupulous in assessing his jurisdiction. Though faced with many requests from some governments and nongovernmental organizations to initiate cases on his own motion, he has refrained from exercising his authority to do so. It seems that the prosecutor is sensitive to the need for a strong perception of the legitimacy of the cases before the Court.

This history is not dispositive, but it is indicative and deserves respect. If the Court has yet to overcome all U.S. doubts, it has acted at nearly every turn in a way that has created no cause for additional doubt or has dispelled initial doubts. Perhaps the Court's record is strong enough so far to say that its actions now deserve the *benefit* of the doubt. The Court will be most effective, however, if it continues to avoid needing such benefit.

Nothing in the operation of the Court to date has raised a red flag for the United States. Hypothesized concerns about a Court fundamentally inimical to U.S. interests have proved unfounded. A policy of cooperation would be a new chapter in U.S. relations with the ICC, but one that would carry no great risk for the United States. There is no particular reason to think that the Court will take a drastically wrong turn, but if it does, a policy of cooperation, including its component particulars, can be reassessed accordingly.

The record of the Court justifies a policy of active U.S. cooperation in furtherance of the U.S. interest in holding perpetrators of atrocities to account. Moreover, there are potential ancillary benefits to U.S. interests from a policy of active cooperation. Of direct relevance would be the contribution the United States could make as an observer to the Assembly of State Parties, which is currently deliberating questions of considerable interest to the United States, such as a definition of and jurisdictional procedure for the crime of "aggression" and issues left open for the 2010 Review Conference mandated by the Rome Statute. The United States will also be in a position to ascertain through participation the openness of the Court and its members to U.S. cooperation and U.S. ideas about the pursuit of international justice more broadly and the operation of the Court in particular.

There may be indirect benefits to U.S. interests as well. U.S. allies would welcome a change to a policy of cooperation, for example. To the extent that international criticism of U.S. detainee policy has harmed American standing, a new policy of cooperation with the ICC could be an important element in restoring it.

Does the performance of the Court justify moving quickly toward ratification of the Rome Statute? We do not think so. Many of the reasons that led us cumulatively to this conclusion have little to do with the operation of the Court so far, and we will soon turn to them, but some do bear directly on the questions about the Court that remain open.

The Court's record is strong but not long. A major review conference will take place in 2010, for example, and the issues that come up there and their resolution are of considerable interest to the United States.

The Court has had only one prosecutor, for example, and this powerful office has been the locus for much of the U.S. concern from the outset. The current prosecutor's nine-year term expires in 2012, and the process the Assembly of State Parties employs in determining a successor (the prosecutor is ineligible for reappointment) will also be of great interest to the United States.

As noted, the prosecutor has so far declined to act on his own motion. It seems unlikely that the prosecutor will *never* act on his own motion—and for that matter, unlikely that the United States would be opposed in all instances if the prosecutor used his power to initiate a case. The question of what circumstances warrant the prosecutor's initiation of a *propriu motu* case and how to build support for the legitimacy of such a case are matters of keen interest to the United States.

Also, as noted, the United States needs to know how welcome its policy of cooperation will be and how receptive the Court will be to U.S. ideas. There is no way to answer such questions theoretically; they are empirical questions, and the United States needs answers to them. In any case, it is important now for the United States to state its views clearly and to be heard at negotiations in which important decisions about the future of the Court are being made.

In addition, there are domestic political reasons for delaying consideration of ratification. The Court remains controversial in the United States, and a divisive Senate debate over ratification, the outcome of which is uncertain, would be unwelcome. Ideally, if the United States is ever to become a State Party to the Rome Statute, the treaty should command strong bipartisan support. The two-thirds hurdle in the Senate is high in its own right, but no one should favor an outcome in which the treaty is approved with exactly sixty-seven votes, the overwhelming majority of which come from a single party. Whether a decision to pursue ratification goes forward or not, members of Congress will want to inform themselves thoroughly on the Court and its operation, and this will take time. The public also needs a better understanding of the subject, especially how the Court fits into the broader theme we have been exploring, international justice, or, if you prefer, the pursuit of accountability for perpetrators of atrocities.

CHAPTER SIX

RECOMMENDATIONS FOR WASHINGTON

End Hostility and Cooperate

THE UNITED STATES should cease its hostility to the International Criminal Court, adopting instead a policy of cooperation with the institution and its mission. For too long the options toward the Court have been framed as ratifying the Rome Statute or actively opposing it. That is a false choice. There is a range of ways in which the United States can cooperate effectively with the Court without ratifying the statute and subjecting the United States to the Court's jurisdiction. A decision on deepening U.S. cooperation, including whether to seek Senate approval of the Rome Statute, and if so, when, ought to await a full review by the administration and the Senate and the outcome of the 2010 Review Conference. This issue is addressed in greater detail below. In the meantime, the United States can and should realign its policy toward the Court in many ways. We offer some illustrative recommendations for consideration by the Executive Branch and Congress. Of course, a policy of cooperation is a mutual endeavor that takes into account the needs and capabilities of the cooperating parties, in this case the United States and the Court. The policy of greater cooperation we recommend for the United States implies a dialogue in which Washington and the Court determine the best ways to work together.

The avenues for cooperation include:

—expressing presidential-level support for the Court's mission, while strengthening protections for U.S. personnel

—establishing a congressionally mandated commission to review the operation of the Court since its founding in 2003

—protecting and assisting victims of heinous crimes

—helping to build judicial capacity to prosecute war criminals in other countries so that they do not have to resort to the ICC

—contributing to the further establishment of a credible international institution

—supporting the Court's investigations

In each of these areas, the United States has a number of practical options, which are detailed below. The potential for cooperation can best be seen in the Darfur case.

Express Support for the Court's Mission

Even when opposing the Court, the United States has stated consistently that it shares its values, such as a commitment to ending impunity and the prevention of grave crimes. U.S. moral support can be made concrete in myriad ways, beginning with a clear statement of policy such as a presidential decision directive or executive order that formally ends U.S. hostility toward the Court and outlines a series of steps the United States will take to enhance the Court's effectiveness and, more broadly, to help ensure perpetrators of mass atrocities are brought to justice. These steps should include in the first instance decisions to:

—"re-sign" the Rome Statute

—designate a senior U.S. official as the focal point for ICC policymaking

—establish a congressionally mandated task force to review the operation of the Court in order to build support for possible U.S. ratification

—as a further protection for U.S. personnel, take legislative and other steps to ensure that there is no gap, perceived or otherwise, in U.S. authority, capacity, and intention to prosecute those within its jurisdiction accused of perpetrating mass atrocities and other war crimes

—participate actively in the 2010 Review Conference of the Rome Statute and the debate on the crime of aggression

—coordinate with allies to promote accountability

—voice U.S. support for using the Security Council to refer atrocities to the Court

—support a future multinational referral of grave crimes to the Court for investigation

—establish a post at the U.S. Mission to the UN with responsibility for Court-related issues

—sign the Agreement on Privileges and Immunities of the ICC

"Re-sign" the Rome Statute.

Although principally a symbolic gesture, the easiest and most direct step to express support for the Court's mission would be to "re-sign" the Rome Statute. The United States can do so simply by sending a letter to UN Secretary-General Ban Ki-moon withdrawing the May 6, 2002, letter to Secretary-General Kofi Annan by Under Secretary John Bolton. Such a simple step is all that is required because the principal effect of the prior letter, also known as the "Bolton letter," was merely to signal the previous administration's intention *not* "to become a party to the treaty." Although the Bolton letter was directed to the secretary-general because of the United Nations' role as the treaty's depository, there is no protocol laying out such a procedure; the letter merely served as a means of notice. Accordingly, a new letter to the secretary-general withdrawing the old one would provide such notice in reverse.

Just as the Bolton letter was intended as a signal to the rest of the world of the Bush administration's opposition to international institutions it believed would limit American influence and leverage, a decision to nullify the Bolton letter would send a potent signal of Washington's willingness to work cooperatively with international institutions aligned with broad American interests.

Designate a senior-level official as the focal point
for policymaking on the ICC.

Implementing the changes we recommend requires that there be a senior-level official in Washington with the clear lead for setting and coordinating policy on the ICC.

Establish a congressionally mandated commission to
review the operation of the Court since 2003.

Although we believe that consideration of ratification is premature, we also believe it is in the United States' interest to build a strong relationship with the Court that leaves U.S. options open down the road. This will require educating Congress and the public on the workings of the Court since it opened for business. To that end, the president should recommend that Congress authorize an independent bipartisan task force to assess the operation of the Court, with a focus on the specific areas of concern expressed by government officials of both parties. A similar effort on U.S.-UN relations, co-chaired by former Senate majority leader George Mitchell and former speaker of the House Newt Gingrich, helped forge bipartisan agreement on an important range of UN-related issues, including, for the first time, the premise that "perpetrators must be held accountable for war crimes and crimes against humanity."[1]

Strengthen protections for U.S. personnel.

The administration should authorize the Departments of Justice and Defense to conduct a joint review of U.S. laws with the aim of ensuring that there is no gap, intentional or otherwise, in U.S. law that might be exploited in an effort to prosecute U.S. personnel. Some of this is already under way in the passage by Congress of the Genocide Accountability Act (GAA) and the Child Soldiers Protection and Accountability Act, both of which address specific ICC provisions. The measures were adopted unanimously in the Senate and House and signed into law by President Bush in 2007 and 2008, respectively. Congress has also been working to pass an accountability act that would address trafficking in persons. In addition, the United States should provide a dossier for its own purposes, making clear that its own citizens are beyond the statutory reach of the ICC, affirming the principle of complementarity incorporated in the treaty, and affirming the demonstrated ability, record, and intention of the United States to identify, investigate, and prosecute anyone under its jurisdiction suspected of committing atrocity crimes. Since the strictures under the American Service-Members' Protection Act (ASPA) have been waived, relegislated, or overtaken by events, it is probably unnecessary to open the political can of worms that would come from a frontal effort to repeal the legislation or to redraft it in its entirety. Any additional issues arising out of ASPA can likely be resolved by executive order or legislative language on a modest scale. Legislative efforts should instead focus on ensuring that U.S. servicemen and -women and others face no legitimate risk of being called before the ICC on the pretext that the U.S. lacks the legal authority, capacity, or intention to prosecute atrocity crimes to the fullest extent of the law. In addition, the president should direct the secretary of defense to undertake a detailed review of the operation of the military justice system to verify "complementarity" under the standards of the Rome Statute.

Participate in the 2010 Review Conference and rejoin debate on the crime of aggression.

The United States should participate as an observer at the Review Conference of the Rome Statute, which is set for the first half of 2010. On the agenda will be the status of Article 124 (a poorly drafted opt-out provision for State Parties), as well as the crime of aggression. To prepare, the United States should immediately rejoin the informal discussions on the crime of aggression. The definition of a crime of aggression, its triggering mechanism, and how the amendment will enter into force are sure to be key issues at the Review Conference, and the result will have an impact on U.S. interests. Because these issues remain disputed, the United States would benefit from joining the debate.

At the informal meetings to discuss the definition of aggression, the United States should strongly endorse a triggering mechanism for the crime of aggression that requires action by the UN Security Council. To be sure, such a proposal is not new: the U.S. delegation at the Rome Conference criticized the treaty's failure at that time to tie the prosecutor's ability to prosecute the crime of aggression to a Security Council resolution authorizing him to do so. The issue was not resolved in Rome, however, and the United States voiced skepticism about including aggression in the statute at all, citing the lack of consensus on its definition. By voicing support for one of the proposals on the table to codify the crime of aggression, albeit one that reserves determinations of aggression for the Security Council, U.S. officials would nonetheless signal an important shift in policy—one that accepts the definition of aggression that State Parties and the international community have worked for five years to achieve but remains committed to a dispositive role for the Security Council on issues of war and peace.

Voice support for using the Security Council to refer atrocities to the Court.

The United States also could move beyond the statement it made when it abstained on the Darfur referral, voicing full support for using the Security Council to refer cases to the Court. During the Darfur vote in the Security Council, the United States reiterated many of its objections to the Court. This language focused on past debates rather than future cooperation and demonstrated a reluctance to embrace the Court as a viable institution for promoting international justice. The United States should no longer maintain such a reluctant stance. Although the Court's jurisdiction over non-party nationals has long been a concern for the United States, the U.S. position has been that, when possible, the Security Council should be the body to confer jurisdiction on the Court. The United States ought to adopt a position that Security Council referral is a preferred option (though taking note that there may be instances in which UNSC agreement is not possible). The text of the Darfur referral can serve as a model for future such referrals. Accordingly, the United States should encourage the Security Council to refer cases to the Court and support State Parties working through the Council. By doing so, the United States would promote the role of the Security Council in the Court's affairs, put pressure on reluctant Security Council members that may be tempted to block or slow action, and broadcast Washington's support of the Court's role in promoting international justice.

Coordinate with allies to ensure a united front against impunity. As the Darfur case has shown, even when the Security Council refers a situation to the Court for investigation and prosecution, the Court's efforts cannot succeed without the cooperation and support of the international community. The United States can play a critical role in fostering this cooperation by coordinating with allies on matters of policy toward the Court and its investigations. Whenever possible, this coordination should seek to harmonize national government positions on the difficult challenges facing the Court, such as when the UN should invoke its power to defer investigations. The Darfur case is again a prime example: The Sudanese government has for many years successfully exploited divergent approaches to the Darfur case taken by the United States and others, delaying and hindering the investigation there. Although these efforts to obstruct the prosecutor's progress have now failed, the potential exists for transatlantic divisions to hinder this and future cases. Accordingly, the United States and its partners should make all efforts to resolve policy disputes about the Court's cases through internal diplomatic channels and, in public, present a united front against impunity.

Consider supporting a future multinational referral of grave crimes to the Court for investigation. Realistically, it is all too likely that there will come a time when the United States and like-minded states on a particular matter will find the path of a referral to the ICC by the Security Council blocked because of a threat of a veto by one of the permanent members. The United States should spare no effort to achieve a Council resolution, but if timely action is impossible, the United States should consider joining like-minded State Parties to the Court in requesting that the prosecutor initiate an investigation on his own motion.

Establish a post at the U.S. Mission to the United Nations with responsibility for Court-related issues.

The diplomatic efforts identified above could be promoted by establishing a specific position at the U.S. Mission to the United Nations with responsibility for Court-related issues. Such a move would stop short of appointing a permanent representative to the Court, as is often done with independent international organizations, while at the same time signaling an interest in working with the Court's representatives at the UN.

Sign the Agreement on Privileges and Immunities of the ICC.

Even without ratifying the Rome Statute, the United States could sign the Agreement on Privileges and Immunities of the ICC, which provides privileges and immunities similar to those enjoyed by other international institutions, such as the United Nations. Specifically, it applies to persons conducting business before, and on behalf of, the Court. This includes representatives of State Parties, the prosecutor, judges, and the registrar, as well as defense counsel, witnesses, victims, and experts, among others. The move would be significant because it would allow the United States to formally recognize the Court as an independent international organization entitled to conduct its affairs without undue interference.

Protect and Assist Victims of Heinous Crimes

The cause of international justice is not an abstract notion for the United States; Washington has taken real steps throughout its history to protect victims of mass atrocities. This tradition can continue through constructive engagement with the Court. The options to do so include (i) contributing to the Trust Fund for Victims; (ii) providing support to victims who need protection or are otherwise vulnerable; and (iii) enacting a visa program for victims of crimes under investigation by the Court.

Contribute to the Trust Fund for Victims.

The trust fund, established by Article 79 of the Rome Statute, benefits victims of grave crimes within the Court's jurisdiction, which, in practice, means the situations formally identified by the prosecutor. It does so by raising awareness of the situation of victims, mobilizing resources to rebuild their lives and their communities, advocating for reconciliation after violent conflicts, and implementing reparation orders made by the Court. Because of its mission, the Trust Fund for Victims solicits voluntary contributions from governments, organizations, corporations, and individuals. A contribution by the United States would be especially timely, as the trust fund announced in 2008 an appeal to raise €10 million to assist victims of sexual violence.

Notably, although the Rome Statute also created the Trust Fund for Victims, it is independent from the Court and probably is not subject to the restrictions in ASPA, which refers specifically to the "International Criminal Court." And appropriations already may be available. The Torture Victims Relief Act authorizes the U.S. Agency for International Development (USAID) to provide $13 million annually "for direct services to victims of torture."

*Provide support to victims who need protection
or are vulnerable.*

The United States could take an active role in the protection of victims of crimes under investigation by the Court. Because the Court is investigating atrocities as they occur, such as the ongoing genocide in Darfur, protecting victims is a tall order. In 2007, the Victims and Witnesses Unit at the Court "saw a six-fold increase in the number of individuals referred for protection and nearly a four-fold increase in the number of individuals admitted into [its] Protection Program," according to a recent report.[2] These efforts could benefit from diplomatic and other assistance from the United States.

*Consider a visa program for witnesses
and victims of crimes under investigation by the Court.*

The Refugee Crisis in Iraq Act was signed into law in 2008, providing 5,000 new visas for refugees fleeing violence in Iraq. A similar targeted program for witnesses and those who survived the "most serious crimes of concern to the international community as a whole" would reaffirm America's role as a leading defender of human rights. The State Department's Bureau of Population, Refugees, and Migration is well placed to manage such an effort, as it has extensive experience with complex refugee emergencies and a strong relationship with UNHCR (the Office of the United Nations High Commissioner for Refugees). The United States should also actively encourage its allies and others to undertake similar programs.

Promote Complementarity by Building Global Judicial Capacity

As a court of last resort, the scope of the International Criminal Court's jurisdiction is defined in large part by the ability and willingness of states to combat impunity. The United States can play a positive role in both respects. As a practical matter, this can include: (i) offering technical assistance programs to enhance the capacity of states to prosecute grave crimes; and (ii) applying diplomatic pressure on target states to encourage domestic prosecution.

*Offer technical assistance to enhance states'
capacity to prosecute grave crimes.*

The United States could play a lead role in ensuring that domestic judicial systems are capable of prosecuting grave crimes. The State Department, the U.S. Agency for International Development, and the Department of Justice already fund hundreds of millions of dollars worth of programs to support the rule of law through technical assistance programs and grants. The American Bar Association's Rule of Law Initiative, the United States Institute of Peace, the National Democratic Institute, the International Republican Institute, and other similar groups already have programs in place to help countries revise their criminal codes, develop independent judiciaries, and advance competent domestic policing. With a little change in emphasis, this funding could include programs to promote the adoption of prohibitions on genocide, war crimes, and crimes against humanity, as well as to remove domestic barriers to prosecution for these crimes, such as statutes of limitations and broad immunity provisions for government officials.

The grants described above could be provided first to those who signed Article 98 agreements with the United States. This prioritization would reward these countries for their cooperation in a manner that nonetheless would promote the overriding goal of ending impunity for perpetrators of these crimes.

Apply diplomatic pressure on target states to encourage domestic prosecution of grave crimes.

Just as technical assistance grants can help states develop the ability to combat impunity, diplomatic pressure can develop their will to do so. Accordingly, the United States could apply pressure on target states—those that might be subject to a Court-led investigation—to themselves investigate grave crimes committed on their territory and prosecute those who are responsible. For example, the prosecutor has undertaken an analysis of the situation in Colombia, where the United States has national interests. What the United States should be doing, knowing that the prosecutor is analyzing the situation in Colombia, is to press Bogotá to make good on its promises of accountability.

Reaffirm the principle of respect for the decisions of states to join the Court or not to join.

Officially, U.S. policy is to respect other nations' decisions to join the Court and ask that they respect the U.S. decision not to become a member at this time. Practically, however, there are legitimate questions about whether this is true. Some point to Iraq. In 2005, the Iraqi Transitional Government decided in a January cabinet meeting to join the Court. After the announcement was made public in February, the government quickly changed course; reports suggest that the United States applied pressure to encourage a reversal. Given this history, and the U.S.

troop presence and relationship with the Iraqi government, the United States could demonstrate that it meant what it said by expressing support for Iraq's accession to the Rome Statute, if and when it chooses to do so.

Contribute to Building a Credible Institution

The United States could seek to reduce its concerns about the Court's lack of oversight and potential for prosecutorial misconduct by supporting efforts to build institutional checks and balances, as well as strong links to other international bodies. This includes: (i) supporting the creation of an independent Office of Inspector General; and (ii) supporting the work of the ICC Liaison Office at the UN.

Support the creation of an independent Office of Inspector General.

The United States could support the efforts of the Assembly of States Parties (ASP) to create an independent oversight mechanism, such as an Office of Inspector General. Although the Rome Statute provided for such a body in Article 112, member states have yet to create one. The State Parties recognize the importance of an independent oversight mechanism, noting in a recent report that the Court was vulnerable to criticism without such a mechanism. There is some discussion that an amendment to the Rome Statute would be needed to create the mechanism, placing it squarely on the agenda of the Review Conference. If that happens, the United States could be an important voice. With an oversight body still in the planning stages, the United States has an opportunity to help shape its contours. For example, although there is a proposal for an independent oversight office to open in

November 2009, there is no agreement yet on exactly what sorts of misconduct or allegations it would investigate or to whom it would report and be accountable.

The United States could support calls for a strong Office of Inspector General, housed at the United Nations in New York but accountable jointly to—and financed jointly by—the Assembly of States Parties and the UN General Assembly. The Office of Inspector General could have a broad mandate to investigate allegations ranging from routine staff misconduct to more serious abuses of the Court's investigative and prosecutorial functions. And its responsibilities could include annual reports to the UN Security Council to assist the Council to exercise the powers bestowed on it by the Rome Statute. Beyond proposals for how the oversight mechanism should operate most effectively, U.S. support for an Office of Inspector General could include financial contributions and personnel; the symbolism of an American-funded office, or an office led in good faith by an American, would not be lost on the Court or its member states.

If the United States attends the Review Conference in 2010, the creation or strengthening of this office could be a constructive issue for Washington to address.

Support the work of the ICC Liaison Office at the UN.
The United States could support the work of the ICC Liaison Office to the United Nations, which was established in 2005 to coordinate the Court's relationship with the UN, State Party missions in New York, and nonmember states. Specifically, the United States could sign a memorandum of understanding with the Liaison Office, permitting it to operate as an independent international organization in New York. At present, the office is situated at the United Nations with the status of an independent observer;

this classification was necessary owing to Washington's tenuous relationship with the Court. In addition, the United States could encourage the office to expand and play a larger role in the Court's external affairs. Right now, the office is staffed by a single mid-level official, who is responsible for working on behalf of all of the Court's organs. A larger office, with more senior leadership and clear lines of communication with the Court's officials, could strengthen the relationship between the Court and the United Nations, as well as with nations in the UN General Assembly that remain outside the Assembly of States Parties.

Support the Court's Investigations

The cases presently before the Court involve unquestionably serious crimes, and the perpetrators facing justice in The Hague are exactly the kinds of criminals the United States has long sought to bring to justice. To assist these admirable efforts, the United States could take concrete steps to support the prosecutor's work. Whether at the investigative stage or at trial, these could include: (i) sharing intelligence, including satellite photos and signal intercepts; (ii) contributing investigative personnel, such as forensic experts; (iii) providing logistical support and ad hoc security assistance to ICC investigative teams in the field; (iv) crafting an extradition treaty to send fugitives to the Court; and (v) appointing liaisons with ICC investigators in selected situation countries.

Share intelligence, including satellite photos and signal intercepts.

The United States could share intelligence with the prosecutor, including satellite photos and signal intercepts, to assist the investigation of crimes under the Court's jurisdiction and to prove cases at trial. The Court's rules permit the prosecutor to enter confidentiality agreements with governments for exactly this purpose, allowing the prosecutor access to valuable leads in his cases while protecting national intelligence services' sources and methods. Satellite photos and signal intercepts can be particularly important to investigations of mass crimes like genocide. Aerial photographs can demonstrate the scope of atrocities and document the movement of troops. Similarly, signal intercepts often are essential to prove the involvement of senior officials in crimes committed by their subordinates; in fact, such evidence was among the proof upon which the prosecutor built his case against the leaders of the Lord's Resistance Army in Uganda.

Although such intelligence is closely held, the Court has a record of keeping sensitive information safe. The Clinton administration reached agreements with the International Criminal Tribunal for Rwanda (ICTR) and the International Criminal Tribunal for the former Yugoslavia (ICTY) in the mid-1990s on the conveyance of classified information. The U.S. government has thus developed both legal documentation and experience to arrange for such intelligence cooperation. In 2007, the prosecutor finalized security arrangements with the European Union to provide it with access to classified information. This agreement is likely to be one of many, with bilateral arrangements focusing on specific situations being the most common form of investigative cooperation.

Contribute investigative personnel, such as forensic experts.
The United States could take another practical step to help the prosecutor pursue cases by contributing experts to his investigations. Personnel in the FBI, Bureau of Alcohol, Tobacco, and Firearms (ATF), military, intelligence community, and elsewhere in the federal government possess unrivaled expertise in forensics,

such as DNA analysis, fingerprint examination, ballistics testing, weapons systems identification and tracking, computer science, and assessments of communication systems. The United States could offer the services of these experts on a case-by-case basis when they would play a key role in bringing perpetrators of grave crimes to justice.

Provide logistical support and ad hoc security assistance to ICC investigative teams in the field.

The United States also could use its substantial logistical expertise to assist the Court's investigators in the field. As the slate of cases before the Court has made clear, atrocity crimes often are committed in areas disconnected from the rest of the world, whether by a lack of communication lines or the stark realities of geography. Investigations on the ground in Darfur, northern Uganda, Congo, and the Central African Republic require immense logistical support to be effective. At the same time, these areas are susceptible to rapid shifts in the security situation. The United States could help the Court with both challenges. For example, the U.S. military and aid agencies could consult with Court personnel to help them plan safe investigative missions, provide access to communication tools such as voice and video links, and help arrange transport into and out of areas that otherwise would be inaccessible. Similarly, if Court personnel find themselves in danger, the U.S. military and aid agencies could work with other states and international organizations to take them out of harm's way.

Craft an extradition treaty to send fugitives to the Court.

The United States could craft an extradition treaty to send fugitives to the Court once a warrant for their arrest has been issued.

The move would not be unprecedented. In 1996, Congress enacted legislation to implement executive agreements with the International Criminal Tribunals for Yugoslavia and Rwanda that provided for the arrest and surrender of fugitives indicted by these courts if they were found in the United States. With this statute already on the books, amending it to include the International Criminal Court would be a straightforward, albeit potentially controversial, move.

Appoint liaisons with ICC investigators in selected situation countries.

To facilitate the sorts of practical assistance outlined above, the United States could appoint liaisons with ICC investigators in selected countries, such as Uganda, Afghanistan, and Colombia. These countries are either the subject of investigations by the prosecutor or could be soon, and the United States has a substantial presence in each. Appointing an individual to receive requests from the Court's investigators and manage any assistance would not only build a positive working relationship with the Court but also signal a willingness to promote international justice.

THE POTENTIAL FOR COOPERATION IN THE DARFUR CASE

The United States could pursue many of the options detailed above to assist the fight against impunity in Darfur. For example, it could contribute to the Trust Fund for Victims to support rehabilitative programs for victims in Darfur and apply diplomatic pressure on Sudan to prosecute lower-level offenders in domestic courts. A stronger ICC Liaison Office at the UN could provide Security Council members with more timely and detailed information about the progress of the case, allowing the Council to conduct a full debate on the propriety of an Article 16 deferral. And the prosecutor's investigation could benefit greatly from U.S. support. If the United States shared intelligence with the Court, it might strengthen the case against President Bashir: aerial photographs of Darfur, for example, could demonstrate the scope of the atrocities and document the movement of government-aligned forces; signals intelligence and wire intercepts could potentially provide confirmation of Bashir's role in the genocide. At the same time, the United States could contribute investigative expertise—for example, tracing the origin of weapons used by the Janjaweed in its attacks.

Legislative changes would be necessary to pursue some of these options. Although the next administration could take many of the steps detailed above without congressional action, some legislative changes would be necessary to pursue them all. The waiver provisions contained in ASPA permit the president to cooperate with the Court under certain conditions, so long as he makes the requisite findings.

We grant that there are some who will remain implacably opposed to the Court. We respect their position. We would encourage them to remain open-minded on the practical question of what to do about some of the world's worst offenders. It is possible to oppose the ICC in principle; but, especially in light of the fact that the Security Council acted to grant the Court jurisdiction over Sudan, the prospect of holding the perpetrators of atrocities to account at the ICC would seem to be welcome. The same argument is warranted in the cases of indicted fugitives Kony, Ntganda, Harun, and Kushayb. Would it be better for any of them to escape accountability for their crimes than to be brought before the ICC?

In any case, the best principles of the United States lie on the side of, one way or another, getting these people rather than letting them get away.

THE ISSUE OF RATIFICATION

As discussed above, it is premature to submit the Rome Statute to the Senate for advice and consent to ratification. At this writing, the United States has yet to formally reverse its policy of hostility to the Court and has not even begun to pursue the various options for intensive and cooperative engagement with the Court, many potential avenues of which are outlined here.

Ending the formal policy of hostility to the Court and firmly placing the United States behind the Court and its missions is the next essential step in realigning U.S. policy toward the Court. Before making a decision on whether it is in either the United States' or the Court's interest for the United States to become a party, the United States should undertake the formal congressionally mandated review outlined in this report.

In addition, the United States should take full part in the debate on aggression and participate actively as a non-party observer in the 2010 Review Conference as part of the process of considering the future question of ratification.

A decision on deepening U.S. cooperation, including whether or when to seek Senate approval of the Rome Statute, ought to await a full review by the U.S. Senate and the administration, including the reports of these groups, and the outcome of the 2010 Review Conference.

In the meantime, we recommend that Congress undertake fact-finding missions to evaluate the operation of the ICC firsthand. These should include but certainly not be limited to visits to the

Court's headquarters in The Hague. Members of Congress should also familiarize themselves with the stories of the victims of the world's worst crimes, visit the places where they have occurred, and attend ceremonies in which the plight of victims is memorialized. We expect that the more familiar members of Congress and those concerned become with these stories, the more outspokenly committed they will be to a reaffirmation of the deeply ingrained American principle of justice for all.

Rome Statute of the International Criminal Court

Excerpted text of the Rome Statute circulated as document A/CONF.183/9 of 17 July 1998 and corrected by process-verbaux of 10 November 1998, 12 July 1999, 30 November 1999, 8 May 2000, 17 January 2001 and 16 January 2002. The Statute entered into force on 1 July 2002.

Preamble

The States Parties to this Statute,

Conscious that all peoples are united by common bonds, their cultures pieced together in a shared heritage, and concerned that this delicate mosaic may be shattered at any time,

Mindful that during this century millions of children, women and men have been victims of unimaginable atrocities that deeply shock the conscience of humanity,

Recognizing that such grave crimes threaten the peace, security and well-being of the world,

Affirming that the most serious crimes of concern to the international community as a whole must not go unpunished and that their effective prosecution must be ensured by taking measures at the national level and by enhancing international cooperation,

Determined to put an end to impunity for the perpetrators of these crimes and thus to contribute to the prevention of such crimes,

Recalling that it is the duty of every State to exercise its criminal jurisdiction over those responsible for international crimes,

Reaffirming the Purposes and Principles of the Charter of the United Nations, and in particular that all States shall refrain from the threat or use of force against the territorial integrity or political independence of any State, or in any other manner inconsistent with the Purposes of the United Nations,

Emphasizing in this connection that nothing in this Statute shall be taken as authorizing any State Party to intervene in an armed conflict or in the internal affairs of any State,

Determined to these ends and for the sake of present and future generations, to establish an independent permanent International Criminal Court in relationship with the United Nations system, with jurisdiction over the most serious crimes of concern to the international community as a whole,

Emphasizing that the International Criminal Court established under this Statute shall be complementary to national criminal jurisdictions,

Resolved to guarantee lasting respect for and the enforcement of international justice,

Have agreed as follows:

Part I Establishment of the Court

Article 1
The Court
An International Criminal Court ('the Court') is hereby established. It shall be a permanent institution and shall have the power to exercise its jurisdiction over persons for the most serious crimes of international concern, as referred to in this Statute, and shall be complementary to national

criminal jurisdictions. The jurisdiction and functioning of the Court shall be governed by the provisions of this Statute. . . .

Part II Jurisdiction, admissibility and applicable law

Article 5
Crimes within the jurisdiction of the Court

1. The jurisdiction of the Court shall be limited to the most serious crimes of concern to the international community as a whole. The Court has jurisdiction in accordance with this Statute with respect to the following crimes:

    (a) The crime of genocide;

    (b) Crimes against humanity;

    (c) War crimes;

    (d) The crime of aggression.

2. The Court shall exercise jurisdiction over the crime of aggression once a provision is adopted in accordance with articles 121 and 123 defining the crime and setting out the conditions under which the Court shall exercise jurisdiction with respect to this crime. Such a provision shall be consistent with the relevant provisions of the Charter of the United Nations.

Article 6
Genocide

For the purpose of this Statute, 'genocide' means any of the following acts committed with intent to destroy, in whole or in part, a national, ethnical, racial or religious group, as such:

    (a) Killing members of the group;

    (b) Causing serious bodily or mental harm to members of the group;

    (c) Deliberately inflicting on the group conditions of life calculated to bring about its physical destruction in whole or in part;

    (d) Imposing measures intended to prevent births within the group;

    (e) Forcibly transferring children of the group to another group.

Article 7
Crimes against humanity

1. For the purpose of this Statute, 'crime against humanity' means any of the following acts when committed as part of a widespread or systematic attack directed against any civilian population, with knowledge of the attack:

(a) Murder;

(b) Extermination;

(c) Enslavement;

(d) Deportation or forcible transfer of population;

(e) Imprisonment or other severe deprivation of physical liberty in violation of fundamental rules of international law;

(f) Torture;

(g) Rape, sexual slavery, enforced prostitution, forced pregnancy, enforced sterilization, or any other form of sexual violence of comparable gravity;

(h) Persecution against any identifiable group or collectivity on political, racial, national, ethnic, cultural, religious, gender as defined in paragraph 3, or other grounds that are universally recognized as impermissible under international law, in connection with any act referred to in this paragraph or any crime within the jurisdiction of the Court;

(i) Enforced disappearance of persons;

(j) The crime of apartheid;

(k) Other inhumane acts of a similar character intentionally causing great suffering, or serious injury to body or to mental or physical health. . . .

Article 8
War crimes

1. The Court shall have jurisdiction in respect of war crimes in particular when committed as part of a plan or policy or as part of a large-scale commission of such crimes.

2. For the purpose of this Statute, "war crimes" means:

(a) Grave breaches of the Geneva Conventions of 12 August 1949, namely, any of the following acts against persons or property protected under the provisions of the relevant Geneva Convention:

(i) Willful killing;

(ii) Torture or inhuman treatment, including biological experiments;

(iii) Willfully causing great suffering, or serious injury to body or health;

(iv) Extensive destruction and appropriation of property, not justified by military necessity and carried out unlawfully and wantonly;

(v) Compelling a prisoner of war or other protected person to serve in the forces of a hostile Power;

(vi) Willfully depriving a prisoner of war or other protected person of the rights of fair and regular trial;

(vii) Unlawful deportation or transfer or unlawful confinement;

(viii) Taking of hostages. . . .

(b) Other serious violations of the laws and customs applicable in international armed conflict, within the established framework of international law. . . .

(c) In the case of an armed conflict not of an international character, serious violations of article 3 common to the four Geneva Conventions of 12 August 1949. . . .

(d) Paragraph 2 (c) applies to armed conflicts not of an international character and thus does not apply to situations of internal disturbances and tensions, such as riots, isolated and sporadic acts of violence or other acts of a similar nature.

(e) Other serious violations of the laws and customs applicable in armed conflicts not of an international character, within the established framework of international law. . . .

(f) Paragraph 2 (e) applies to armed conflicts not of an international character and thus does not apply to situations of internal disturbances and tensions, such as riots, isolated and sporadic acts of violence or other acts of a similar nature. It applies to armed conflicts that take place in the territory of a State when there is protracted armed conflict between governmental authorities and organized armed groups or between such groups.

3. Nothing in paragraph 2 (c) and (e) shall affect the responsibility of a Government to maintain or re-establish law and order in the State or to defend the unity and territorial integrity of the State, by all legitimate means. . . .

Article 11
Jurisdiction ratione temporis

1. The Court has jurisdiction only with respect to crimes committed after the entry into force of this Statute.

2. If a State becomes a Party to this Statute after its entry into force, the Court may exercise its jurisdiction only with respect to crimes committed after the entry into force of this Statute for that State, unless that State has made a declaration under article 12, paragraph 3.

Article 12
Preconditions to the exercise of jurisdiction

1. A State which becomes a Party to this Statute thereby accepts the jurisdiction of the Court with respect to the crimes referred to in article 5.

2. In the case of article 13, paragraph (a) or (c), the Court may exercise its jurisdiction if one or more of the following States are Parties to this Statute or have accepted the jurisdiction of the Court in accordance with paragraph 3:

(a) The State on the territory of which the conduct in question occurred or, if the crime was committed on board a vessel or aircraft, the State of registration of that vessel or aircraft;

(b) The State of which the person accused of the crime is a national.

3. If the acceptance of a State which is not a Party to this Statute is required under paragraph 2, that State may, by declaration lodged with the Registrar, accept the exercise of jurisdiction by the Court with respect to the crime in question. The accepting State shall cooperate with the Court without any delay or exception in accordance with Part 9.

Article 13
Exercise of jurisdiction

The Court may exercise its jurisdiction with respect to a crime referred to in article 5 in accordance with the provisions of this Statute if:

(a) A situation in which one or more of such crimes appears to have been committed is referred to the Prosecutor by a State Party in accordance with article 14;

(b) A situation in which one or more of such crimes appears to have been committed is referred to the Prosecutor by the Security Council acting under Chapter VII of the Charter of the United Nations; or

(c) The Prosecutor has initiated an investigation in respect of such a crime in accordance with article 15.

Article 14
Referral of a situation by a State Party

1. A State Party may refer to the Prosecutor a situation in which one or more crimes within the jurisdiction of the Court appear to have been committed requesting the Prosecutor to investigate the situation for the purpose of determining whether one or more specific persons should be charged with the commission of such crimes.

2. As far as possible, a referral shall specify the relevant circumstances and be accompanied by such supporting documentation as is available to the State referring the situation.

Article 15
Prosecutor

1. The Prosecutor may initiate investigations *proprio motu* on the basis of information on crimes within the jurisdiction of the Court.

2. The Prosecutor shall analyze the seriousness of the information received. For this purpose, he or she may seek additional information from States, organs of the United Nations, intergovernmental or non-governmental organizations, or other reliable sources that he or she deems appropriate, and may receive written or oral testimony at the seat of the Court.

3. If the Prosecutor concludes that there is a reasonable basis to proceed with an investigation, he or she shall submit to the Pre-Trial Chamber a request for authorization of an investigation, together with any supporting material collected. Victims may make representations to the Pre-Trial Chamber, in accordance with the Rules of Procedure and Evidence.

4. If the Pre-Trial Chamber, upon examination of the request and the supporting material, considers that there is a reasonable basis to proceed with an investigation, and that the case appears to fall within the juris-

diction of the Court, it shall authorize the commencement of the investigation, without prejudice to subsequent determinations by the Court with regard to the jurisdiction and admissibility of a case.

5. The refusal of the Pre-Trial Chamber to authorize the investigation shall not preclude the presentation of a subsequent request by the Prosecutor based on new facts or evidence regarding the same situation.

6. If, after the preliminary examination referred to in paragraphs 1 and 2, the Prosecutor concludes that the information provided does not constitute a reasonable basis for an investigation, he or she shall inform those who provided the information. This shall not preclude the Prosecutor from considering further information submitted to him or her regarding the same situation in the light of new facts or evidence.

Article 16
Deferral of investigation or prosecution

No investigation or prosecution may be commenced or proceeded with under this Statute for a period of 12 months after the Security Council, in a resolution adopted under Chapter VII of the Charter of the United Nations, has requested the Court to that effect; that request may be renewed by the Council under the same conditions.

Article 17
Issues of admissibility

1. Having regard to paragraph 10 of the Preamble and article 1, the Court shall determine that a case is inadmissible where:

(a) The case is being investigated or prosecuted by a State which has jurisdiction over it, unless the State is unwilling or unable genuinely to carry out the investigation or prosecution;

(b) The case has been investigated by a State which has jurisdiction over it and the State has decided not to prosecute the person concerned, unless the decision resulted from the unwillingness or inability of the State genuinely to prosecute;

(c) The person concerned has already been tried for conduct which is the subject of the complaint, and a trial by the Court is not permitted under article 20, paragraph 3;

(d) The case is not of sufficient gravity to justify further action by the Court.

2. In order to determine unwillingness in a particular case, the Court shall consider, having regard to the principles of due process recognized by international law, whether one or more of the following exist, as applicable:

(a) The proceedings were or are being undertaken or the national decision was made for the purpose of shielding the person concerned from criminal responsibility for crimes within the jurisdiction of the Court referred to in article 5;

(b) There has been an unjustified delay in the proceedings which in the circumstances is inconsistent with an intent to bring the person concerned to justice;

(c) The proceedings were not or are not being conducted independently or impartially, and they were or are being conducted in a manner which, in the circumstances, is inconsistent with an intent to bring the person concerned to justice.

3. In order to determine inability in a particular case, the Court shall consider whether, due to a total or substantial collapse or unavailability of its national judicial system, the State is unable to obtain the accused or the necessary evidence and testimony or otherwise unable to carry out its proceedings. . . .

Article 20
Ne bis in idem

1. Except as provided in this Statute, no person shall be tried before the Court with respect to conduct which formed the basis of crimes for which the person has been convicted or acquitted by the Court.

2. No person shall be tried by another court for a crime referred to in article 5 for which that person has already been convicted or acquitted by the Court.

3. No person who has been tried by another court for conduct also proscribed under article 6, 7 or 8 shall be tried by the Court with respect to the same conduct unless the proceedings in the other court:

(a) Were for the purpose of shielding the person concerned from criminal responsibility for crimes within the jurisdiction of the Court; or

(b) Otherwise were not conducted independently or impartially in accordance with the norms of due process recognized by international law and were conducted in a manner which, in the circumstances, was inconsistent with an intent to bring the person concerned to justice. . . .

Article 54
Duties and powers of the Prosecutor with respect to investigations

1. The Prosecutor shall:

(a) In order to establish the truth, extend the investigation to cover all facts and evidence relevant to an assessment of whether there is criminal responsibility under this Statute, and, in doing so, investigate incriminating and exonerating circumstances equally;

(b) Take appropriate measures to ensure the effective investigation and prosecution of crimes within the jurisdiction of the Court, and in doing so, respect the interests and personal circumstances of victims and witnesses, including age, gender as defined in article 7, paragraph 3, and health, and take into account the nature of the crime, in particular where it involves sexual violence, gender violence or violence against children; and

(c) Fully respect the rights of persons arising under this Statute.

2. The Prosecutor may conduct investigations on the territory of a State:

(a) In accordance with the provisions of Part 9; or

(b) As authorized by the Pre-Trial Chamber under article 57, paragraph 3 (d).

3. The Prosecutor may:

(a) Collect and examine evidence;

(b) Request the presence of and question persons being investigated, victims and witnesses;

(c) Seek the cooperation of any State or intergovernmental organization or arrangement in accordance with its respective competence and/or mandate;

(d) Enter into such arrangements or agreements, not inconsistent with this Statute, as may be necessary to facilitate the cooperation of a State, intergovernmental organization or person;

(e) Agree not to disclose, at any stage of the proceedings, documents or information that the Prosecutor obtains on the condition of confidentiality and solely for the purpose of generating new evidence, unless the provider of the information consents; and

(f) Take necessary measures, or request that necessary measures be taken, to ensure the confidentiality of information, the protection of any person or the preservation of evidence. . . .

Article 56
Role of the Pre-Trial Chamber in relation to a unique investigative opportunity

1. (a) Where the Prosecutor considers an investigation to present a unique opportunity to take testimony or a statement from a witness or to examine, collect or test evidence, which may not be available subsequently for the purposes of a trial, the Prosecutor shall so inform the Pre-Trial Chamber.

(b) In that case, the Pre-Trial Chamber may, upon request of the Prosecutor, take such measures as may be necessary to ensure the efficiency and integrity of the proceedings and, in particular, to protect the rights of the defence.

(c) Unless the Pre-Trial Chamber orders otherwise, the Prosecutor shall provide the relevant information to the person who has been arrested or appeared in response to a summons in connection with the investigation referred to in subparagraph (a), in order that he or she may be heard on the matter.

2. The measures referred to in paragraph 1 (b) may include:

(a) Making recommendations or orders regarding procedures to be followed;

(b) Directing that a record be made of the proceedings;

(c) Appointing an expert to assist;

(d) Authorizing counsel for a person who has been arrested, or appeared before the Court in response to a summons, to participate, or where there has not yet been such an arrest or appearance or counsel has not been designated, appointing another counsel to attend and represent the interests of the defence;

(e) Naming one of its members or, if necessary, another available judge of the Pre-Trial or Trial Division to observe and make recommendations or orders regarding the collection and preservation of evidence and the questioning of persons;

(f) Taking such other action as may be necessary to collect or preserve evidence.

3.(a) Where the Prosecutor has not sought measures pursuant to this article but the Pre-Trial Chamber considers that such measures are required to preserve evidence that it deems would be essential for the defence at trial, it shall consult with the Prosecutor as to whether there is good reason for the Prosecutor's failure to request the measures. If upon consultation, the Pre-Trial Chamber concludes that the Prosecutor's failure to request such measures is unjustified, the Pre-Trial Chamber may take such measures on its own initiative.

(b) A decision of the Pre-Trial Chamber to act on its own initiative under this paragraph may be appealed by the Prosecutor. The appeal shall be heard on an expedited basis.

4. The admissibility of evidence preserved or collected for trial pursuant to this article, or the record thereof, shall be governed at trial by article 69, and given such weight as determined by the Trial Chamber.

Article 57
Functions and powers of the Pre-Trial Chamber

1.Unless otherwise provided in this Statute, the Pre-Trial Chamber shall exercise its functions in accordance with the provisions of this article.

2 . (a) Orders or rulings of the Pre-Trial Chamber issued under articles 15, 18, 19, 54, paragraph 2, 61, paragraph 7, and 72 must be concurred in by a majority of its judges.

(b) In all other cases, a single judge of the Pre-Trial Chamber may exercise the functions provided for in this Statute, unless otherwise provided for in the Rules of Procedure and Evidence or by a majority of the Pre-Trial Chamber.

3.In addition to its other functions under this Statute, the Pre-Trial Chamber may:

(a) At the request of the Prosecutor, issue such orders and warrants as may be required for the purposes of an investigation;

(b)Upon the request of a person who has been arrested or has appeared pursuant to a summons under article 58, issue such orders, including measures such as those described in article 56, or seek such cooperation pursuant to Part 9 as may be necessary to assist the person in the preparation of his or her defence;

(c) Where necessary, provide for the protection and privacy of victims and witnesses, the preservation of evidence, the protection of persons who have been arrested or appeared in response to a summons, and the protection of national security information;

(d) Authorize the Prosecutor to take specific investigative steps within the territory of a State Party without having secured the cooperation of that State under Part 9 if, whenever possible having regard to the views of the State concerned, the Pre-Trial Chamber has determined in that case that the State is clearly unable to execute a request for cooperation due to the unavailability of any authority or any component of its judicial system competent to execute the request for cooperation under Part 9.

(e) Where a warrant of arrest or a summons has been issued under article 58, and having due regard to the strength of the evidence and the rights of the parties concerned, as provided for in this Statute and the Rules of Procedure and Evidence, seek the cooperation of States pursuant to article 93, paragraph 1 (k), to take protective measures for the purpose of forfeiture, in particular for the ultimate benefit of victims. . . .

Article 64
Functions and powers of the Trial Chamber

1. The functions and powers of the Trial Chamber set out in this article shall be exercised in accordance with this Statute and the Rules of Procedure and Evidence.

2. The Trial Chamber shall ensure that a trial is fair and expeditious and is conducted with full respect for the rights of the accused and due regard for the protection of victims and witnesses.

3. Upon assignment of a case for trial in accordance with this Statute, the Trial Chamber assigned to deal with the case shall:

(a) Confer with the parties and adopt such procedures as are necessary to facilitate the fair and expeditious conduct of the proceedings;

(b) Determine the language or languages to be used at trial; and

(c) Subject to any other relevant provisions of this Statute, provide for disclosure of documents or information not previously disclosed, sufficiently in advance of the commencement of the trial to enable adequate preparation for trial.

4. The Trial Chamber may, if necessary for its effective and fair functioning, refer preliminary issues to the Pre-Trial Chamber or, if necessary, to another available judge of the Pre-Trial Division.

5. Upon notice to the parties, the Trial Chamber may, as appropriate, direct that there be joinder or severance in respect of charges against more than one accused.

6. In performing its functions prior to trial or during the course of a trial, the Trial Chamber may, as necessary:

(a) Exercise any functions of the Pre-Trial Chamber referred to in article 61, paragraph 11;

(b) Require the attendance and testimony of witnesses and production of documents and other evidence by obtaining, if necessary, the assistance of States as provided in this Statute;

(c) Provide for the protection of confidential information;

(d) Order the production of evidence in addition to that already collected prior to the trial or presented during the trial by the parties;

(e) Provide for the protection of the accused, witnesses and victims; and

(f) Rule on any other relevant matters.

7. The trial shall be held in public. The Trial Chamber may, however, determine that special circumstances require that certain proceedings be in closed session for the purposes set forth in article 68, or to protect confidential or sensitive information to be given in evidence.

8. (a) At the commencement of the trial, the Trial Chamber shall have read to the accused the charges previously confirmed by the Pre-Trial Chamber. The Trial Chamber shall satisfy itself that the accused understands the nature of the charges. It shall afford him or her the opportu-

nity to make an admission of guilt in accordance with article 65 or to plead not guilty.

(b) At the trial, the presiding judge may give directions for the conduct of proceedings, including to ensure that they are conducted in a fair and impartial manner. Subject to any directions of the presiding judge, the parties may submit evidence in accordance with the provisions of this Statute.

9. The Trial Chamber shall have, *inter alia*, the power on application of a party or on its own motion to:

(a) Rule on the admissibility or relevance of evidence; and

(b) Take all necessary steps to maintain order in the course of a hearing.

10. The Trial Chamber shall ensure that a complete record of the trial, which accurately reflects the proceedings, is made and that it is maintained and preserved by the Registrar. . . .

Article 67
Rights of the accused

1. In the determination of any charge, the accused shall be entitled to a public hearing, having regard to the provisions of this Statute, to a fair hearing conducted impartially, and to the following minimum guarantees, in full equality:

(a) To be informed promptly and in detail of the nature, cause and content of the charge, in a language which the accused fully understands and speaks;

(b) To have adequate time and facilities for the preparation of the defence and to communicate freely with counsel of the accused's choosing in confidence;

(c) To be tried without undue delay;

(d) Subject to article 63, paragraph 2, to be present at the trial, to conduct the defence in person or through legal assistance of the accused's choosing, to be informed, if the accused does not have legal assistance, of this right and to have legal assistance assigned by the Court in any case where the interests of justice so require, and without payment if the accused lacks sufficient means to pay for it;

(e) To examine, or have examined, the witnesses against him or her and to obtain the attendance and examination of witnesses on his or her behalf under the same conditions as witnesses against him or her. The accused shall also be entitled to raise defences and to present other evidence admissible under this Statute;

(f) To have, free of any cost, the assistance of a competent interpreter and such translations as are necessary to meet the requirements of fairness, if any of the proceedings of or documents presented to the Court are not in a language which the accused fully understands and speaks;

(g) Not to be compelled to testify or to confess guilt and to remain silent, without such silence being a consideration in the determination of guilt or innocence;

(h) To make an unsworn oral or written statement in his or her defence; and

(i) Not to have imposed on him or her any reversal of the burden of proof or any onus of rebuttal.

2. In addition to any other disclosure provided for in this Statute, the Prosecutor shall, as soon as practicable, disclose to the defence evidence in the Prosecutor's possession or control which he or she believes shows or tends to show the innocence of the accused, or to mitigate the guilt of the accused, or which may affect the credibility of prosecution evidence. In case of doubt as to the application of this paragraph, the Court shall decide.

Article 68
Protection of the victims and witnesses and their participation in the proceedings

1. The Court shall take appropriate measures to protect the safety, physical and psychological well-being, dignity and privacy of victims and witnesses. In so doing, the Court shall have regard to all relevant factors, including age, gender as defined in article 7, paragraph 3, and health, and the nature of the crime, in particular, but not limited to, where the crime involves sexual or gender violence or violence against children. The Prosecutor shall take such measures particularly during the investigation and prosecution of such crimes. These measures shall not be prejudicial

to or inconsistent with the rights of the accused and a fair and impartial trial.

2. As an exception to the principle of public hearings provided for in article 67, the Chambers of the Court may, to protect victims and witnesses or an accused, conduct any part of the proceedings *in camera* or allow the presentation of evidence by electronic or other special means. In particular, such measures shall be implemented in the case of a victim of sexual violence or a child who is a victim or a witness, unless otherwise ordered by the Court, having regard to all the circumstances, particularly the views of the victim or witness.

3. Where the personal interests of the victims are affected, the Court shall permit their views and concerns to be presented and considered at stages of the proceedings determined to be appropriate by the Court and in a manner which is not prejudicial to or inconsistent with the rights of the accused and a fair and impartial trial. Such views and concerns may be presented by the legal representatives of the victims where the Court considers it appropriate, in accordance with the Rules of Procedure and Evidence.

4. The Victims and Witnesses Unit may advise the Prosecutor and the Court on appropriate protective measures, security arrangements, counselling and assistance as referred to in article 43, paragraph 6.

5. Where the disclosure of evidence or information pursuant to this Statute may lead to the grave endangerment of the security of a witness or his or her family, the Prosecutor may, for the purposes of any proceedings conducted prior to the commencement of the trial, withhold such evidence or information and instead submit a summary thereof. Such measures shall be exercised in a manner which is not prejudicial to or inconsistent with the rights of the accused and a fair and impartial trial.

6. A State may make an application for necessary measures to be taken in respect of the protection of its servants or agents and the protection of confidential or sensitive information. . . .

Article 74
Requirements for the decision

1. All the judges of the Trial Chamber shall be present at each stage of the trial and throughout their deliberations. The Presidency may, on a

case-by-case basis, designate, as available, one or more alternate judges to be present at each stage of the trial and to replace a member of the Trial Chamber if that member is unable to continue attending.

2. The Trial Chamber's decision shall be based on its evaluation of the evidence and the entire proceedings. The decision shall not exceed the facts and circumstances described in the charges and any amendments to the charges. The Court may base its decision only on evidence submitted and discussed before it at the trial.

3. The judges shall attempt to achieve unanimity in their decision, failing which the decision shall be taken by a majority of the judges.

4. The deliberations of the Trial Chamber shall remain secret.

5. The decision shall be in writing and shall contain a full and reasoned statement of the Trial Chamber's findings on the evidence and conclusions. The Trial Chamber shall issue one decision. When there is no unanimity, the Trial Chamber's decision shall contain the views of the majority and the minority. The decision or a summary thereof shall be delivered in open court. . . .

Article 79
Trust Fund

1. A Trust Fund shall be established by decision of the Assembly of States Parties for the benefit of victims of crimes within the jurisdiction of the Court, and of the families of such victims.

2. The Court may order money and other property collected through fines or forfeiture to be transferred, by order of the Court, to the Trust Fund.

3. The Trust Fund shall be managed according to criteria to be determined by the Assembly of States Parties. . . .

Article 98
Cooperation with respect to waiver of immunity and consent to surrender

1. The Court may not proceed with a request for surrender or assistance which would require the requested State to act inconsistently with its obligations under international law with respect to the State or diplomatic immunity of a person or property of a third State, unless the Court

can first obtain the cooperation of that third State for the waiver of the immunity.

2. The Court may not proceed with a request for surrender which would require the requested State to act inconsistently with its obligations under international agreements pursuant to which the consent of a sending State is required to surrender a person of that State to the Court, unless the Court can first obtain the cooperation of the sending State for the giving of consent for the surrender. . . .

Article 112
Assembly of States Parties

1. An Assembly of States Parties to this Statute is hereby established. Each State Party shall have one representative in the Assembly who may be accompanied by alternates and advisers. Other States which have signed this Statute or the Final Act may be observers in the Assembly.

2. The Assembly shall:

(a) Consider and adopt, as appropriate, recommendations of the Preparatory Commission;

(b) Provide management oversight to the Presidency, the Prosecutor and the Registrar regarding the administration of the Court;

(c) Consider the reports and activities of the Bureau established under paragraph 3 and take appropriate action in regard thereto;

(d) Consider and decide the budget for the Court;

(e) Decide whether to alter, in accordance with article 36, the number of judges;

(f) Consider pursuant to article 87, paragraphs 5 and 7, any question relating to non-cooperation;

(g) Perform any other function consistent with this Statute or the Rules of Procedure and Evidence.

3.(a) The Assembly shall have a Bureau consisting of a President, two Vice-Presidents and 18 members elected by the Assembly for three-year terms.

(b) The Bureau shall have a representative character, taking into account, in particular, equitable geographical distribution and the adequate representation of the principal legal systems of the world.

(c) The Bureau shall meet as often as necessary, but at least once a year. It shall assist the Assembly in the discharge of its responsibilities.

4. The Assembly may establish such subsidiary bodies as may be necessary, including an independent oversight mechanism for inspection, evaluation and investigation of the Court, in order to enhance its efficiency and economy.

5. The President of the Court, the Prosecutor and the Registrar or their representatives may participate, as appropriate, in meetings of the Assembly and of the Bureau.

6. The Assembly shall meet at the seat of the Court or at the Headquarters of the United Nations once a year and, when circumstances so require, hold special sessions. Except as otherwise specified in this Statute, special sessions shall be convened by the Bureau on its own initiative or at the request of one third of the States Parties.

7. Each State Party shall have one vote. Every effort shall be made to reach decisions by consensus in the Assembly and in the Bureau. If consensus cannot be reached, except as otherwise provided in the Statute:

(a) Decisions on matters of substance must be approved by a two-thirds majority of those present and voting provided that an absolute majority of States Parties constitutes the quorum for voting;

(b) Decisions on matters of procedure shall be taken by a simple majority of States Parties present and voting.

8. A State Party which is in arrears in the payment of its financial contributions towards the costs of the Court shall have no vote in the Assembly and in the Bureau if the amount of its arrears equals or exceeds the amount of the contributions due from it for the preceding two full years. The Assembly may, nevertheless, permit such a State Party to vote in the Assembly and in the Bureau if it is satisfied that the failure to pay is due to conditions beyond the control of the State Party.

9. The Assembly shall adopt its own rules of procedure.

10. The official and working languages of the Assembly shall be those of the General Assembly of the United Nations. . . .

Article 120
Reservations

No reservations may be made to this Statute.

Article 121
Amendments

1. After the expiry of seven years from the entry into force of this Statute, any State Party may propose amendments thereto. The text of any proposed amendment shall be submitted to the Secretary-General of the United Nations, who shall promptly circulate it to all States Parties.

2. No sooner than three months from the date of notification, the Assembly of States Parties, at its next meeting, shall, by a majority of those present and voting, decide whether to take up the proposal. The Assembly may deal with the proposal directly or convene a Review Conference if the issue involved so warrants.

3. The adoption of an amendment at a meeting of the Assembly of States Parties or at a Review Conference on which consensus cannot be reached shall require a two-thirds majority of States Parties.

4. Except as provided in paragraph 5, an amendment shall enter into force for all States Parties one year after instruments of ratification or acceptance have been deposited with the Secretary-General of the United Nations by seven-eighths of them.

5. Any amendment to articles 5, 6, 7 and 8 of this Statute shall enter into force for those States Parties which have accepted the amendment one year after the deposit of their instruments of ratification or acceptance. In respect of a State Party which has not accepted the amendment, the Court shall not exercise its jurisdiction regarding a crime covered by the amendment when committed by that State Party's nationals or on its territory.

6. If an amendment has been accepted by seven-eighths of States Parties in accordance with paragraph 4, any State Party which has not accepted the amendment may withdraw from this Statute with immediate effect, notwithstanding article 127, paragraph 1, but subject to article 127, paragraph 2, by giving notice no later than one year after the entry into force of such amendment.

7. The Secretary-General of the United Nations shall circulate to all States Parties any amendment adopted at a meeting of the Assembly of States Parties or at a Review Conference. . . .

Article 123
Review of the Statute

1. Seven years after the entry into force of this Statute the Secretary-General of the United Nations shall convene a Review Conference to consider any amendments to this Statute. Such review may include, but is not limited to, the list of crimes contained in article 5. The Conference shall be open to those participating in the Assembly of States Parties and on the same conditions.

2. At any time thereafter, at the request of a State Party and for the purposes set out in paragraph 1, the Secretary-General of the United Nations shall, upon approval by a majority of States Parties, convene a Review Conference.

3. The provisions of article 121, paragraphs 3 to 7, shall apply to the adoption and entry into force of any amendment to the Statute considered at a Review Conference.

Article 124
Transitional Provision

Notwithstanding article 12, paragraphs 1 and 2, a State, on becoming a party to this Statute, may declare that, for a period of seven years after the entry into force of this Statute for the State concerned, it does not accept the jurisdiction of the Court with respect to the category of crimes referred to in article 8 when a crime is alleged to have been committed by its nationals or on its territory. A declaration under this article may be withdrawn at any time. The provisions of this article shall be reviewed at the Review Conference convened in accordance with article 123, paragraph 1. . . .

Signing Statement of President Bill Clinton

Statement by U.S. President Bill Clinton,
Authorizing the U.S. signing of the
Rome Statute of the International Criminal Court

31 December 2000
Camp David, Maryland, United States

The United States is today signing the 1998 Rome Treaty on the International Criminal Court. In taking this action, we join more than 130 other countries that have signed by the December 31, 2000 deadline established in the Treaty. We do so to reaffirm our strong support for international accountability and for bringing to justice perpetrators of genocide, war crimes, and crimes against humanity. We do so as well because we wish to remain engaged in making the ICC an instrument of impartial and effective justice in the years to come.

The United States has a long history of commitment to the principle of accountability, from our involvement in the Nuremberg tribunals that brought Nazi war criminals to justice, to our leadership in the effort to establish the International Criminal Tribunals for the Former Yugoslavia and Rwanda. Our action today sustains that tradition of moral leadership.

Under the Rome Treaty, the International Criminal Court (ICC) will come into being with the ratification of 60 governments, and will have jurisdiction over the most heinous abuses that result from international conflict, such as war crimes, crimes against humanity, and genocide. The Treaty requires that the ICC not supersede or interfere with functioning national judicial systems; that is, the ICC Prosecutor is authorized to take action against a suspect only if the country of nationality is unwilling or unable to investigate allegations of egregious crimes by their national. The U.S. delegation to the Rome Conference worked hard to achieve these limitations, which we believe are essential to the international credibility and success of the ICC.

In signing, however, we are not abandoning our concerns about significant flaws in the Treaty. In particular, we are concerned that when the Court comes into existence, it will not only exercise authority over personnel of states that have ratified the Treaty, but also claim jurisdiction over personnel of states that have not. With signature, however, we will be in a position to influence the evolution of the Court. Without signature, we will not.

Signature will enhance our ability to further protect U.S. officials from unfounded charges and to achieve the human rights and accountability objectives of the ICC. In fact, in negotiations following the Rome Conference, we have worked effectively to develop procedures that limit the likelihood of politicized prosecutions. For example, U.S. civilian and military negotiators helped to ensure greater precision in the definitions of crimes within the Court's jurisdiction.

But more must be done. Court jurisdiction over U.S. personnel should come only with U.S. ratification of the Treaty. The United States should have the chance to observe and assess the functioning of the Court, over time, before choosing to become subject to its jurisdiction. Given these concerns, I will not, and do not recommend that my successor submit the Treaty to the Senate for advice and consent until our fundamental concerns are satisfied.

Nonetheless, signature is the right action to take at this point. I believe that a properly constituted and structured International Criminal Court would make a profound contribution in deterring egregious human rights abuses worldwide, and that signature increases the chances for productive discussions with other governments to advance these goals in the months and years ahead.

"THE BOLTON LETTER"

May 6, 2002

Dear Mr. Secretary-General:

This is to inform you, in connection with the Rome Statute of the International Criminal Court adopted on July 17, 1998, that the United States does not intend to become a party to the treaty. Accordingly, the United States has no legal obligations arising from its signature on December 31, 2000. The United States requests that its intention not to become a party, as expressed in this letter, be reflected in the depositary's status lists relating to this treaty.

Sincerely,
/s/
John R. Bolton

SECURITY COUNCIL RESOLUTION 1593, MARCH 31, 2005

Resolution 1593 (2005)

**Adopted by the Security Council at its
5158th meeting, on 31 March 2005**

The Security Council,

Taking note of the report of the International Commission of Inquiry on violations of international humanitarian law and human rights law in Darfur (S/2005/60),

Recalling article 16 of the Rome Statute under which no investigation or prosecution may be commenced or proceeded with by the International Criminal Court for a period of 12 months after a Security Council request to that effect,

Also recalling articles 75 and 79 of the Rome Statute and encouraging States to contribute to the ICC Trust Fund for Victims,

Taking note of the existence of agreements referred to in Article 98-2 of the Rome Statute,

Determining that the situation in Sudan continues to constitute a threat to international peace and security,

Acting under Chapter VII of the Charter of the United Nations,

1. *Decides* to refer the situation in Darfur since 1 July 2002 to the Prosecutor of the International Criminal Court;

2. *Decides* that the Government of Sudan and all other parties to the conflict in Darfur, shall cooperate fully with and provide any necessary assistance to the Court and the Prosecutor pursuant to this resolution and, while recognizing that States not party to the Rome Statute have no obligation under the Statute, urges all States and concerned regional and other international organizations to cooperate fully;

3. *Invites* the Court and the African Union to discuss practical arrangements that will facilitate the work of the Prosecutor and of the Court, including the possibility of conducting proceedings in the region, which would contribute to regional efforts in the fight against impunity;

4. *Also encourages* the Court, as appropriate and in accordance with the Rome Statute, to support international cooperation with domestic efforts to promote the rule of law, protect human rights and combat impunity in Darfur;

5. *Also emphasizes* the need to promote healing and reconciliation and encourages in this respect the creation of institutions, involving all sectors of Sudanese society, such as truth and/or reconciliation commissions, in order to complement judicial processes and thereby reinforce the efforts to restore long-lasting peace, with African Union and international support as necessary;

6. *Decides* that nationals, current or former officials or personnel from a contributing State outside Sudan which is not a party to the Rome Statute of the International Criminal Court shall be subject to the exclusive jurisdiction of that contributing State for all alleged acts or omissions arising out of or related to operations in Sudan established or authorized by the Council or the African Union, unless such exclusive jurisdiction has been expressly waived by that contributing State;

7. *Recognizes* that none of the expenses incurred in connection with the referral including expenses related to investigations or prosecutions in connection with that referral, shall be borne by the United Nations

and that such costs shall be borne by the parties to the Rome Statute and those States that wish to contribute voluntarily;

8. *Invites* the Prosecutor to address the Council within three months of the date of adoption of this resolution and every six months thereafter on actions taken pursuant to this resolution;

9. *Decides* to remain seized of the matter.

Security Council Resolution 1828, July 31, 2008

Resolution 1828 (2008)

Adopted by the Security Council at its
5947th meeting, on 31 July 2008

The Security Council,

Reaffirming all its previous resolutions and presidential statements concerning the situation in Sudan,

Reaffirming its strong commitment to the sovereignty, unity, independence and territorial integrity of Sudan and its determination to work with the Government of Sudan, in full respect of its sovereignty, to assist in tackling the various challenges in Sudan,

Recalling also its previous resolutions 1325 (2000) and 1820 (2008) on women, peace and security, 1502 (2003) on the protection of humanitarian and United Nations personnel, 1612 (2005) on children and armed conflict and the subsequent conclusions on the Sudan of the Working Group on Children in Armed Conflicts (S/AC.51/2008/7) as approved by the Council, and 1674 (2006) on the protection of civilians in armed conflict, which reaffirms inter alia the relevant provisions of the United Nations World Summit outcome document, as well as the report of its Mission to Sudan from 3 to 6 June 2008,

Welcoming the report of the Secretary-General and the Chairperson of the African Union Commission of 7 July 2008 (S/2008/443), and *recalling* the confirmation of President Bashir during his meeting with the Council that UNAMID shall be deployed in full,

Deploring, one year after the adoption of resolution 1769 (2007), the deterioration in the security and humanitarian situation in Darfur,

Stressing the need to enhance the safety and security of UNAMID personnel,

Noting with strong concern ongoing attacks on the civilian population and humanitarian workers and continued and widespread sexual violence, including as outlined in the reports of the Secretary-General,

Emphasizing the need to bring to justice the perpetrators of such crimes and *urging* the Government of Sudan to comply with its obligations in this respect, and *reiterating* its condemnation of all violations of human rights and international humanitarian law in Darfur,

Taking note of the African Union (AU) communiqué of the 142nd Peace and Security Council (PSC) Meeting dated 21 July (S/2008/481, annex), *having in mind* concerns raised by members of the Council regarding potential developments subsequent to the application by the Prosecutor of the International Criminal Court of 14 July 2008, and *taking note* of their intention to consider these matters further,

Reaffirming its concern that the ongoing violence in Darfur might further negatively affect the stability of Sudan as a whole as well as the region, *noting with concern* the ongoing tensions between the Governments of Sudan and Chad, and *reiterating* that a reduction in these tensions and rebel activity in both countries must be addressed to achieve long-term peace in Darfur and in the region,

Expressing its determination to promote and support the political process in Darfur, especially the new Chief Mediator, and *deploring* the fact that some groups refuse to join the political process,

Reiterating its deep concern for the decreasing security of humanitarian personnel, including killings of humanitarian workers, in Darfur and the hindering of their access to populations in need, *condemning* the parties to the conflict who have failed to ensure the full, safe and unhindered access of relief personnel as well as the delivery of humanitarian assistance, *further condemning* all instances of banditry and car-jackings, and *recognizing* that with many civilians in Darfur having been displaced humanitarian efforts remain a priority until a sustained ceasefire and inclusive political process are achieved,

Demanding an end to attacks on civilians, from any quarter, including by aerial bombing, and the use of civilians as human shields,

Determining that the situation in Darfur, Sudan continues to constitute a threat to international peace and security,

1. *Decides* to extend the mandate of UNAMID as set out in resolution 1769 (2007) for a further 12 months to 31 July 2009;

2. *Welcomes* the agreement of the Government of Sudan, during its meeting with the Council on 5 June 2008, to the African Union (AU)–United Nations (UN) troop deployment plan; *commends* the contribution made by troop and police contributing countries and donors to UNAMID; and, in order to facilitate the full and successful deployment of UNAMID and to enhance the protection of its personnel, *calls*:

(a) for the rapid deployment, as planned by the Secretary-General, of force enablers, including the Heavy Support Package's engineer, logistic, medical and signal units, and of additional troops, police and civilian personnel including contractors; and

(b) on United Nations Member States to pledge and contribute the helicopter, aerial reconnaissance, ground transport, engineering and logistical units and other force enablers required;

3. *Underlines* the importance of raising the capability of those UNAMID battalions formerly deployed by the African Union Mission in Sudan and other incoming battalions; *requests* the continuing assistance of donors in ensuring that these battalions are trained and equipped to United Nations standards; and further requests the Secretary-General to include this in his next report to the Council;

4. *Welcomes* the intention of the Secretary-General to deploy 80 per cent of UNAMID by 31 December 2008, and urges the Government of Sudan, troop contributors, donors, the United Nations Secretariat and all stakeholders to do all they can to facilitate this;

5. *Welcomes* the signing of the Status of Forces Agreement; *demands* that the Government of Sudan complies with it fully and without delay; and *further demands* that the Government of Sudan and all armed groups in Sudan's territory ensure the full and expeditious deployment of UNAMID and remove all obstacles to the proper discharge of its mandate, including by ensuring its security and freedom of movement;

6. *Underlines*, with a view to strengthening cooperation with troop and police contributors as well as their safety and security, the need for enhanced guidelines, procedures and information-sharing;

7. *Underlines* the need for UNAMID to make full use of its current mandate and capabilities with regard to the protection of civilians, ensuring humanitarian access and working with other United Nations agencies;

8. *Reiterates* its condemnation of previous attacks on UNAMID; *stresses* that any attack or threat on UNAMID is unacceptable; *demands* that there be no recurrence of such attacks, and *further requests* the Secretary-General to report to the Security Council on the result of United Nations investigations and with recommendations to prevent a reoccurrence of such attacks;

9. *Reiterates* there can be no military solution to the conflict in Darfur, and that an inclusive political settlement and the successful deployment of UNAMID are essential to re-establishing peace in Darfur;

10. *Welcomes* the appointment of Mr. Djibrill Yipènè Bassolé as Joint AU-UN Chief Mediator, who has its full support; *calls* on the Government of Sudan and rebel groups to engage fully and constructively in the peace process, including by entering into talks under the mediation of Mr. Bassolé; *demands* all the parties, in particular rebel groups, to finalize their preparations for and to join the talks; and underlines also the need for the engagement of civil society, including women and women-led organizations, community groups and tribal leaders;

11. *Demands* an end to violence by all sides, to attacks on civilians, peacekeepers and humanitarian personnel, and to other violations of human rights and international humanitarian law in Darfur; further *demands* that all parties cease hostilities and immediately commit themselves to a sustained and permanent ceasefire; and encourages the mediation to consult with all relevant parties on security issues with a view to

a more effective ceasefire commission working closely with UNAMID to monitor the cessation of hostilities;

12. *Calls* on Sudan and Chad to abide by their obligations under the Dakar Agreement, the Tripoli Agreement and subsequent bilateral agreements, including by ending support for rebel groups; *welcomes* the creation of the Dakar Agreement Contact Group, and the consideration being given to improved monitoring of the border between Sudan and Chad; and *takes note* of the agreement of Sudan and Chad on 18 July to restore diplomatic relations;

13. *Demands* the full implementation of the Communiqué between the Government of Sudan and the United Nations on Facilitation of Humanitarian Activities in Darfur, and that the Government of Sudan, all militias, armed groups and all other stakeholders ensure the full, safe and unhindered access of humanitarian organizations and relief personnel;

14. *Requests* the Secretary-General to ensure (a) continued monitoring and reporting of the situation of children and (b) continued dialogue with the parties to the conflict towards the preparation of time bound action plans to end the recruitment and use of child soldiers and other violations against children;

15. *Demands* that the parties to the conflict immediately take appropriate measures to protect civilians, including women and children, from all forms of sexual violence, in line with resolution 1820 (2008); and requests the Secretary-General to ensure, as appropriate, that resolutions 1325 (2000) and 1820 are implemented by UNAMID and to include information on this in his report requested in paragraph 16 below;

16. *Demands* that the parties to the conflict in Darfur fulfill their international obligations and their commitments under relevant agreements, this resolution and other relevant Council resolutions;

17. *Requests* the Secretary-General to report to the Council every 60 days after the adoption of this resolution on developments on UNAMID, the political process, the security and humanitarian situation, and all parties' compliance with their international obligations;

18. *Reiterates* its readiness to take action against any party that impedes the peace process, humanitarian assistance or the deployment of UNAMID; and recognizes that due process must take its course;

19. *Decides* to remain seized of the matter.

Notes

CHAPTER ONE

1. The subject matter jurisdiction of the International Criminal Court is formally "genocide, crimes against humanity, war crimes, and aggression." The definition of aggression has yet to be determined by the parties to the Rome Statute.

2. Report of the Task Force on the United Nations, *American Interests and UN Reform* (Washington: United States Institute of Peace, 2005), p. 14. Lee Feinstein served as staff director of the task force. Tod Lindberg led the working group on human rights.

3. Tod Lindberg led the Genocide Prevention Task Force's expert group on international norms and institutions.

4. Lee Feinstein was then a senior fellow at the Council on Foreign Relations.

5. Lee Feinstein was national security director on the staff of the Hillary Clinton campaign. Tod Lindberg was an informal and unpaid foreign policy adviser to the John McCain campaign.

6. See, for example, John R. Bolton, "American Justice and the International Criminal Court" (Washington: American Enterprise Institute, November 3, 2003) (www.aei.org/publications/filter.all, pubID.19407/pub_detail.asp).

7. See, for example, Lee Feinstein, "Darfur and Beyond: What Is Needed to Prevent Mass Atrocities" (New York: Council on Foreign Relations Special Report, January 2007); and Tod Lindberg, "Protect the People," *Washington Times*, September 27, 2005.

CHAPTER TWO

1. Remarks by the president at the opening commemoration of "50 Years after Nuremberg: Human Rights and the Rule of Law," University of Connecticut, October 15, 1995 (http://clinton6.nara.gov/1995/10/1995-10-15-president-at-50-years-after-nuremberg-symposium.html).

2. Lynn Hunt, *Inventing Human Rights* (New York: W. W. Norton, 2007), p. 117.

3. Robert Kagan, *Dangerous Nation: America's Place in the World, from Its Earliest Days to the Dawn of the 20th Century* (New York: Alfred A. Knopf, 2006), p. 42.

4. As quoted in ibid., pp. 52, 65, 72.

5. Ibid., pp. 42, 45, 47.

6. International law at the time authorized any government to capture, try, and hang pirates. Section 8 of Article I of the U.S. Constitution mandated: "The Congress shall have Power . . . To define and punish Piracies and Felonies committed on the high seas, and Offenses against the Law of Nations." Global Security.org, "Barbary Pirates" (2005) (www.globalsecurity.org/military/ops/barbary.htm).

7. Frank Lambert, *The Barbary Wars: American Independence in the Atlantic World* (New York: Hill and Wang, 2005), pp. 4, 9, 42.

8. John Fabian Witt, "Lincoln's Laws of War: How He Built the Code That Bush Attempted to Destroy," *Slate*, February 11, 2009 (www.slate.com/id/2210918/pagenum/a/).

9. Peter Maguire, *Law and War: An American Story* (Columbia University Press, 2000), pp. 36–37.

10. As quoted in ibid., pp. 41–42.

11. Ibid.

12. Ibid., pp. 36, 43–44.

13. As quoted in ibid., pp. 47–49.

14. As quoted in Jackson Nyamuya Maogoto, *War Crimes and Realpolitik* (Boulder, Colo.: Lynne Rienner, 2004), p. 25.

15. As quoted in Maguire, *Law and War*, p. 69.

16. Maogoto, *War Crimes*, p. 26.

17. Ibid., p. 41.

18. Sandra L. Jamison, "A Permanent International Criminal Court: A Proposal That Overcomes Past Objections," *Denver Journal of International Law and Policy* 23 (1994–95): 422.

19. As quoted in Gary Jonathan Bass, *Stay the Hand of Vengeance* (Princeton University Press, 2000), p. 103.

20. As quoted in John P. Cerone, "Dynamic Equilibrium: The Evolution of U.S. Attitudes toward International Criminal Courts and Tribunals," *European Journal of International Law* 18 (2007): 281–82.

21. As quoted in Bass, *Stay the Hand of Vengeance*, pp. 92–99.

22. Ibid., pp. 76–81.

23. Walter Russell Mead, *Special Providence* (New York: Alfred A. Knopf, 2001), p. 9.

24. Bass, *Stay the Hand of Vengeance*, p. 92.

25. John Kane, *Between Virtue and Power* (Yale University Press, 2008), p. 147.

26. As quoted in Bass, *Stay the Hand of Vengeance*, pp. 149–50, 155.

27. As quoted in ibid., pp. 155–56, 164–66.

28. Ibid., p. 172. Parties to the Kellogg-Briand Pact of 1928 "renounce[d war] . . . as an instrument of national policy in their relations with one another." Germany was a party. The treaty contained no enforcement provisions.

29. See Cerone, "Dynamic Equilibrium," pp. 283–84.

30. Bass, *Stay the Hand of Vengeance*, p. 173.

31. Henry King and Theodore Theofrastous, "From Nuremberg to Rome: A Step Backward for U.S. Foreign Policy," *Case Western Reserve Journal of International Law* 31 (Winter 1999): 49.

32. M. Cherif Bassiouni, "From Versailles to Rwanda in Seventy-Five Years: The Need to Establish a Permanent International Criminal Court," *Harvard Human Rights Journal* 10 (1997): 29.

33. Ibid.

34. As quoted in Kingsley Chiedu Moghalu, *Global Justice* (Westport, Conn.: Praeger Security International, 2006), pp. 41–42.

35. See Telford Taylor, *The Anatomy of the Nuremberg Trials: A Personal Memoir* (New York: Alfred Knopf, 1992); and David Scheffer, "Nuremberg Trials," in *Proceedings of the First International Humanitarian Law Dialogs* (Washington: American Society of International Law, 2008), pp. 178–79.

36. See "Victors' Justice, Losers' Justice," chap. 15 in John Dower, *Embracing Defeat: Japan in the Wake of World War II* (New York: W. W. Norton, 2000).

37. As quoted in Cerone, "Dynamic Equilibrium," p. 286.

38. Michael P. Scharf, "The Jury Is Still Out on the Need for an International Criminal Court," *Duke Journal of Comparative & International Law* 1 (1991): 139.

39. William N. Gianaris, "The New World Order and the Need for an International Criminal Court," *Fordham International Law Journal* 16 (1992–93): 94.

40. Cerone, "Dynamic Equilibrium," p. 287.

41. Gianaris, "The New World Order," p. 95.

42. Jamison, "A Permanent International Criminal Court," p. 427.

43. Ibid.

44. Gianaris, "The New World Order," pp. 89–90, 105–08.

45. King and Theofrastous, "From Nuremberg to Rome," p. 70.

46. *Restatement of the Law (Third), Foreign Relations Law of the United States*, American Law Institute (2006), as quoted in John B. Anderson, "An International Criminal Court—An Emerging Idea," *Nova Law Review* 15 (1991): 439–40.

47. Cerone, "Dynamic Equilibrium," p. 287.

48. 101 Cong. 1 sess., H. CON. RES. 66, March 2, 1989 (http://thomas.loc.gov/cgi-bin/query/z?c101:H.CON.RES.66.IH). The legislation also noted that an ICC must "respect the sovereignty of individual nations" and not derogate from "due process" rights.

49. Anderson, "An International Criminal Court," p. 447.

50. Scharf, "The Jury Is Still Out," p. 143.

51. Benjamin B. Ferencz, "An International Criminal Code and Court: Where They Stand and Where They're Going," *Columbia Journal of Transnational Law* 30 (1992): 387.

52. As quoted in King and Theofrastous, "From Nuremberg to Rome," pp. 71–73.

53. Cerone, "Dynamic Equilibrium," p. 288.

54. Victor Peskin, *International Justice in Rwanda and the Balkans* (Cambridge University Press, 2008), p. 189.

55. As quoted in Cerone, "Dynamic Equilibrium," p. 288.

56. Bass, *Stay the Hand of Vengeance*, p. 224.

57. Moghalu, *Global Justice*, p. 157.

58. Ibid., p. 168.

59. Michael Scharf, "The Iraqi High Tribunal," *Journal of International Criminal Justice* 5 (2007): 259–60.

CHAPTER THREE

1. The parameters of U.S. engagement with the Court during this early period were articulated in the Foreign Operations Appropriations Act of 1990, which expressed that "the United States should explore the need for the establishment of an International Court," while cautioning that "the establishment of such a court or courts for the more effective prosecution of international criminals should not derogate from established standards of due process, the rights of the accused to a fair trial and the sovereignty of individual nations." Foreign Operations Appropriations Act of 1990; Section 599E, P.L. 101–513, 104 Stat. 20662067.

2. Remarks by President Clinton to the 52nd Session of the United Nations General Assembly, New York, New York, September 22, 1997 (http://clinton6.nara.gov/1997/09/1997-09-22-president-remarks-to-un-general-assembly.html).

3. See, for example, David J. Scheffer, "Staying the Course with the International Criminal Court," *Cornell International Law Journal* 35, no. 1 (Nov. 2001–Feb. 2002): 47–100.

4. Statement by the president, Camp David, Maryland, December 31, 2000 (http://clinton6.nara.gov/2000/12/2000-12-31-statement-by-president-on-signature-the-icc-treaty.html).

5. We address the substance of these objections in chapters 4 and 5. See also Ambassador David J. Scheffer, "The Constitutionality of the Rome Statute of the International Criminal Court," *Journal of the Criminal Law and Criminology* 98, no. 3 (Spring 2008): 983–1068.

6. The issue is further complicated by the applicability of customary international law in these circumstances.

7. John Bolton, "Why an International Criminal Court Won't Work," *Wall Street Journal*, March 30, 1998.

8. Jeremy A. Rabkin, "A Dangerous Step Closer to an International Criminal Court," AEI Online (Washington), January 1, 2001 (www.aei.org/publications/pubID.12313/pub_detail.asp).

9. The International Court of Justice has long issued rulings on issues of international aggression.

10. See, for example, Ivo Daalder and James Lindsay, *America Unbound: The Bush Revolution in Foreign Policy* (Brookings, 2003).

11. See Thomas Ricks, "U.S. Signs Treaty on War Crimes Tribunal; Pentagon, Republicans Object to Clinton Move," *Washington Post*, January 1, 2001.

12. State Department Press Release: "International Criminal Court: Letter to UN Secretary-General Kofi Annan," May 6, 2002 (see Appendix C). Bolton's sentiment was echoed later that day by Defense Secretary Donald Rumsfeld, who said, "The United States will regard as illegitimate any attempt by the court or state parties to the treaty to assert the ICC's jurisdiction over American citizens." DoD News Release "Secretary Rumsfeld Statement on the ICC Treaty" (www.defenselink.mil/releases/release.aspx?releaseid=3337). A less conspicuous, and less hostile, policy statement from the government was delivered the same day by Under Secretary of State for Political Affairs Marc Grossman at the Center for Strategic and International Studies in Washington (http://www.csis.org/media/csis/events/020506_grossman.pdf). See also John Bolton, *Surrender Is Not an Option: Defending America at the United Nations* (New York: Threshold Editions, 2007), p. 85.

13. A former Bush State Department legal adviser subsequently argued that the Bolton letter was of limited legal significance. See John Bellinger, "The United States and the ICC: Where We've Been and Where We're Going," speech delivered at De Paul University, April 2008.

14. See Serge Schmemann, "U.S. Links Peacekeeping to Immunity from New Court," *New York Times*, June 19, 2002; for background see AMICC: "Peacekeeping and the ICC" (www.amicc.org/usinfo/administration_policy_pkeeping.html).

15. Many believe this was a misapplication of Article 16, on the grounds that the provision was intended to suspend an active investigation against an individual rather than prevent a hypothetical one against a group.

16. Representatives Ron Paul (R-Tex.) and Henry Hyde (R-Ill.) proposed various amendments to withdraw the U.S. signature from the Rome Statute (House Concurrent Resolution 23), restrict the use of any funds from supporting the ICC or its investigations (Defense Appropriations Amendment 408), and take "such steps necessary to prevent the establishment of an International Criminal Court" (House Bill 4169). For an examination of the legislative history of ASPA and related bills, see Lilian V. Faulhaber, "American Servicemembers' Protection Act of 2002," *Harvard Journal on Legislation* 40 (2003): 537–57.

17. The sponsors of the bill bypassed the usual congressional channels and introduced the legislation as an amendment to the "Supplemental Appropriations Act for Further Recovery from and Response to Terrorist Attacks on the United States." See Adam Clymer, "House Panel Approves Measures to Oppose New Global Court," *New York Times*, May 11, 2002.

18. Article 98 (2) of the Rome Statute says the "Court may not proceed with a request for surrender which would require the requested State to act inconsistently with its obligations under international agreements pursuant to which the consent of a sending State is required to surrender a person of that State to the Court."

19. A list of Article 98 agreements is kept by the Georgetown University Law Center library (www.ll.georgetown.edu/guides/article_98.cfm). The most recent agreement, with Montenegro, entered into

force April 19, 2007 (www.state.gov/documents/organization/100234. pdf).

20. Elizabeth Becker, "European Union Urges Aspirants to Rebuff U.S. on World Court," *New York Times,* August 14, 2002.

21. "Presidential Declaration of MERCOSUR's Commitment to the Rome Statute of the International Criminal Court," XXVIII Meeting of the Council of the Common Market, Asunción, June 20, 2005: "Together we adopt a common position for MERCOSUR with regard to Section 2 of Article 98 of the Rome Statute. We commit to not enter into multilateral or bilateral agreements with third States which would affect the jurisdiction of the International Criminal Court or other obligations established in the Rome Statute." Signed by Presidents Nestor Kirchner (Argentina), Luiz Inácio Lula da Silva (Brazil), Nicanor Duarte Frutos (Paraguay), and Tabaré Vázquez (Uruguay). English translation available at www.iccnow.org/documents/MERCOSUR_Decl_BIA_Jun05.pdf.

22. Written communication from John Bellinger to the authors, February 24, 2009.

23. Department of State, "Trip Briefing: Secretary Condoleezza Rice en Route to San Juan, Puerto Rico," March 10, 2006 (www.state.gov/secretary/rm/2006/63001.htm).

24. See "Combat Commander's Military Strategy and Operational Requirements in Review of the FY2007 Defense Budget," Hearing of the Senate Armed Services Committee, March 14, 2006.

25. Department of Defense: "Quadrennial Defense Review Report," February 6, 2005 (www.defenselink.mil/qdr/report/Report20060203.pdf).

26. John Warner National Defense Authorization Act for Fiscal Year 2007, H.R. 5122 §1222 (http://thomas.loc.gov/cgi-bin/query/F?c109:6:./temp/~c109ILDZNv:e1063814:).

27. National Defense Authorization Act for Fiscal Year 2008, H.R. 4986 §1212 (http://thomas.loc.gov/cgi-bin/bdquery/z?d110:H.R.1585:).

28. AMICC: "Congressional Update: Nethercutt Amendment," March 10, 2009 (www.amicc.org/usinfo/congressional.html#nethercutt).

29. Agence France-Presse: "West Sudan's Darfur conflict 'world's greatest humanitarian crisis': UN," March 19, 2004.

30. Secretary of State Colin L. Powell, written remarks before the Senate Foreign Relations Committee, Washington, September 9, 2004.

31. See, for example, Rachel Zoll, "Evangelicals Lobby Bush on Sudan Crisis," Associated Press, October 18, 2006; *Washington Times*: "Evangelicals Urge Darfur Action," October 19, 2006.

32. *Time*, "The 25 Most Influential Evangelicals in America," November 29, 2004 (www.time.com/time/covers/1101050207/photo essay/9.html).

33. Security Council Resolution 1593 (2005) (www.un.org/News/ Press/docs/2005/sc8351.doc.htm).

34. For example, "It is a big mistake for us to grant any validity to international law even when it may seem in our short-term interest to do so—because, over the long term, the goal of those who think that international law really means anything are those who want to constrict the United States." John Bolton, interviewed in *Insight* magazine, August 2, 1999 (www.insightmag.com/news/1999/08/02/SpecialReport/Just-What. Is.A.War.Criminal-215455.shtml).

35. Michael Abramowitz and Colum Lynch, "Darfur Killings Soften Bush's Opposition to International Court," *Washington Post*, October 12, 2008.

36. ICC Press Release, "The Prosecutor of the ICC Opens Investigation in Darfur," The Hague, June 6, 2005 (www.icc-cpi.int/ pressrelease_details&id=107&l=en.html).

37. ICC arrest warrant for Ahmad Haroun: www.icc-cpi.int/ library/cases/ICC-02-05-01-07-2_English.pdf; ICC arrest warrant for Ali Kushayb: www.icc-cpi.int/library/cases/ICC-02-05-01-07-3_English.pdf.

38. Maggie Farley, "Sudan Promotes Militia Leader in Darfur Violence," *Los Angeles Times*, January 22, 2008.

39. ICC Press Release, "ICC Prosecutor Presents Case against Sudanese President, Hassan Ahmad AL BASHIR, for Genocide, Crimes against Humanity and War Crimes in Darfur," The Hague, July 14, 2008 (www.icc-cpi.int/press/pressreleases/406.html).

40. See, for example, Rony Brauman, "The ICC's Bashir Indictment: Law against Peace," *World Politics Review*, July 23, 2008; Julie Flint and Alex de Waal, "Justice off Course in Darfur," *Washington Post*, Op-Ed, June 28, 2008.

41. James Reinl, "Sarkozy Offers Bashir Deal over War Crimes," *The National*, September 23, 2008.

42. "U.S. Toughens Stance against Freezing Indictment of Sudan President," *Sudan Tribune,* August 4, 2008.

43. UN Security Council Resolution 1828 (2008), July 31, 2008. See p. 2 for the offending text, which reads: "Taking note of the African Union (AU) communiqué of the 142nd Peace and Security Council (PSC) Meeting dated 21 July (S/2008/481, annex), having in mind concerns raised by members of the Council regarding potential developments subsequent to the application by the Prosecutor of the International Criminal Court of 14 July 2008, and taking note of their intention to consider these matters further. . . . "

44. John Heilprin, "U.N. Vote OKs Darfur Peacekeeping, but U.S. Abstains over Sudan Leader's Genocide Charges," *ABC News,* July 31, 2008 (http://abcnews.go.com/International/wireStory?id=5493325).

45. USUN Press Release, "Explanation of vote by Ambassador Alejandro Wolff, U.S. Deputy Permanent Representative, on the renewal of the UNAMID mandate, in the Security Council chamber, July 31, 2008" (www.usunnewyork.usmission.gov/press_releases/20080731_209.html).

46. In the wake of Rome 1998, many countries passed legislation to ensure that they could take advantage of the complementarity standards of the ICC. The Canadian Parliament, for example, enacted the Crimes against Humanity and War Crimes Act in July 2000, reinforcing Canada's position on the Rome Statute and enhancing Canada's ability to prosecute war crimes and crimes against humanity under its domestic criminal code.

47. The Genocide Prevention Act of 2007 (www.govtrack.us/congress/bill.xpd?bill=s110-888); the Child Soldiers Prevention and Accountability Act of 2008 (www.govtrack.us/congress/bill.xpd?bill=s110-2135).

48. Namely, Article 7(2)(c) of the Rome Statute.

49. For an overview of what Obama administration officials have stated with respect to the ICC see AMICC, "Administration Update" (www.amicc.org/usinfo/administration.html).

50. Senate Foreign Relations Committee, "Questions for the Record, Senator John Kerry, Nomination of Hillary Rodham Clinton," January 13, 2009 (www.foreignpolicy.com/files/KerryClintonQFRs.pdf).

51. USUN Press Release, "Statement by Ambassador Susan E. Rice, U.S. Permanent Representative, on Respect for International Humanitarian Law, in the Security Council, January 29, 2009" (www.usunnewyork. usmission.gov/press_releases/20090129_020.html).

CHAPTER FOUR

1. The prosecutor could not investigate the crimes in Darfur before the Security Council's action because Sudan is not a State Party to the Rome Statute.

2. Both conflicts are, of course, cross-border as well, with attendant regional consequences.

3. The prosecutor's letter explained that the "Court may not exercise jurisdiction over the crime [of aggression] until a provision has been adopted which defines the crime and sets out the conditions under which the Court may exercise jurisdiction." Letter from the Chief Prosecutor of the International Criminal Court, The Hague, February 9, 2006 (www2. icc-cpi.int/NR/rdonlyres/04D143C8-19FB-466C-AB77-4CDB2FDEBEF7/ 143682/OTP_letter_to_senders_re_Iraq_9_February_2006.pdf).

4. Alex Little, "Don't Let Uganda's War Criminals off the Hook," *Christian Science Monitor*, October 6, 2006 (www.csmonitor.com/2006/ 1006/p09s01-coop.html).

5. Human Rights Watch, "Courting History: The Landmark International Criminal Court's First Years," July 2008, pp. 67–69 (www.hrw.org/en/reports/2008/07/10/courting-history/).

CHAPTER SIX

1. Newt Gingrich and George Mitchell, *American Interests and UN Reform: A Report of the Congressional Task Force on the United Nations* (Washington: United States Institute of Peace, 2005), p. 46.

2. International Bar Association, "Balancing Rights: The ICC at a Procedural Crossroads," Press Release, July 2, 2008.

INDEX